The Courage to Compete

Living with Cerebral Palsy and Following My Dreams

The Courage to Compete

Living with Cerebral Palsy and Following My Dreams

ABBEY CURRAN
with Elizabeth Kaye

HARPER

An Imprint of HarperCollinsPublishers

The Courage to Compete: Living with Cerebral Palsy
and Following My Dreams
Copyright © 2015 by Abbey Curran
All photos courtesy of the author except:
Photos on pages 143–144 courtesy of
Miss Universe, LP, LLLP & Future Productions, LLC.
All rights reserved. Printed in the United States of America.
No part of this book may be used or reproduced in any manner
whatsoever without written permission except in the case
of brief quotations embodied in critical articles and reviews.
For information address HarperCollins Children's Books, a division
of HarperCollins Publishers, 195 Broadway, New York, NY 10007.
www.epicreads.com

Library of Congress Control Number: 2015933523
ISBN 978-0-06-236391-6

Typography by Erin Fitzsimmons
15 16 17 18 19   PC/RRDH   10 9 8 7 6 5 4 3 2 1

First Edition

*I'd like to dedicate this book to all of those who said I couldn't,
who laughed at me and told me to be realistic.
Thank you from the bottom of my heart
for filling me with the determination to prove you wrong
and pursue dreams that I, too, didn't think were possible.
I would never have worked so hard without you!*

CONTENTS

INTRODUCTION

The most amazing moments of my life came at the Miss Iowa USA pageant. I wasn't there to watch the pageant. I was actually there to compete in it. I felt like I must be sleepwalking or dreaming or something because all my life I had wanted to be a beauty queen. When I got picked for the Top Ten, I thought it was the best thing that had ever happened to me in the entire world. Then I got in the Top Two, which was bigger than anything I had ever thought would happen. It had come down to me and just one other girl, though I knew she would win because she was more beautiful than I could ever imagine being. But then I heard the unbelievable words, "The winner for Miss Iowa 2008 is Abbey Curran!"

Honestly, I was so amazed and excited I thought I

might pass out! As the crown was set on my head, my eyes filled to overflowing with tears of gratitude and joy. It was the moment when my dream came true, when my life changed. Above all, it was the moment that confirmed what I had always believed: anything is possible.

Of course, any contestant would have been thrilled. But I wasn't just any contestant. I was the first person with a disability to compete in a major beauty pageant. The fact that I was there at all amazed a lot of people. To tell you the truth, it amazed me, too, because I knew what it had taken to get there.

I was born with cerebral palsy. I walk with a limp—a serious limp—and I drag my left leg behind me. There's no way I could hide those things no matter how much I might try. So I know how horrible it feels to have people prejudge you, to have them assume you don't have a brain just because you happen to walk differently than they do. And I know what it's like to have people stare at you as if you were a weirdo and ask you questions like, "Can you go places by yourself or drive a car?"

I tell them, "Of course I can . . . I can also feed myself and brush my teeth, too!"

Here's the point: There are two words I've always refused to say, and those two words are "I can't." Lots of people have tried to discourage me from doing things I wanted to do, but whenever someone tells me there's no way I can do something, I always say, "Just watch me."

My life is proof that you can do anything you set your mind to doing, as long as you work hard, never give up, and aren't afraid to fail. I'm aware that most people assume I must be severely limited, but the fact is, I have never put limitations on myself. Sometimes I feel like the bumblebee that isn't supposed to fly because its body is too big and its wings are too small, but the bumblebee doesn't know this—it just flies away!

It may seem like I was born with this positive outlook, but that's not the case. All my life, I've had to ignore my nerves and shyness and force myself to move forward; I've had to act as if I believed in myself until I really, actually did. Along the way, I made history when I became Miss Iowa 2008, and competed for the title of Miss USA. More important, when I was still in high school, I established my own pageant for disabled girls. The pageant is called the Miss You Can Do It pageant, and the name totally sums up what I believe.

I'm determined to do whatever I can to break the glass ceiling that hovers over girls in general, and especially girls with challenges like mine. I want to be an advocate for all the challenged girls who have to deal with the same problems I have faced, problems that confront them all the time, that make them feel so different, and hurt so much they can break your heart. One of the many things I've overcome is getting upset about the pitying looks strangers have given me for as long as I can remember. When I'm just going along, minding my own business, I'll hear someone say, "That poor girl."

You can imagine how awful it is when people you've never even met think they know all about you. So when anyone asks what it is like being born with a disability, my answer is "It sucks!" And that's an understatement. CP permeates every aspect of my life. For instance: I'll get out of my car feeling on top of the world, and one minute later, I'll fall smack down on my face in the parking lot; I'm dying to adopt a Saint Bernard but I can't, because a big dog would knock me down; I want so much to hurry over to people and help them cross the street or to open a door for them, but I almost never do because I can't get there in time.

Another thing I really want is to find an amazing husband and have babies, but I've always had to face the fact that guys look past me. For guys, my CP is a total turnoff, though there's no real reason why that should be. Maybe it's because they wonder if they would have to take care of me, but the answer to that is "NO!" Or maybe they wonder if my CP will get worse (another "NO!") or if I'll die early because of it ("NO!"). Can I have babies? YES! Do I need help with anything? NO WAY! But I can't wear a T-shirt that says all of this, so they don't know, they don't ask, and therefore they don't even try.

But as much as I would love to have a date, a boyfriend, a husband, I try not to worry about it. For me, finding a nice, caring man is like finding a needle in a haystack. Sometimes I think I'm not supposed to be married. Maybe I'm meant to do bigger things. Most women dream of getting married and having babies— and don't get me wrong, those things are definitely on my list—but I'm in nursing school now and want to earn my master of science in nursing first. I'd also love to create my own shoe line and create stylish medical devices like wheelchairs and walkers for those who really need them. Most wheelchairs are totally hideous; they're an eyesore. A lot of times, they have the effect of making disabled people look way sicker than they actually are, and that becomes another hurdle for them to get over. Can you imagine if wheelchairs were pretty? What if each one was a reflection of its user's personality? One might be gold and white and delicate—like the kind of chair you'd see in a beautiful home. Another could be bright red with polka-dot upholstery. If that's how wheelchairs were, you'd definitely have a whole different feeling about the people sitting in them!

I'd also love to be a reporter for CNN or HLN. Being on TV has always been one of my biggest dreams. I'd like to be the person sent to the scene to report live whenever there is a story about bullying or about any issues involving people with disabilities. I'd like to be the voice in America for people who aren't usually heard. I'd like to be the person who isn't afraid to state the facts and tell the whole story, no matter how difficult or painful it may be. I want to tell stories about girls who get bullied because they wear leg braces or because they're born with Down syndrome or because they had chemotherapy and lost their hair. I want to help people understand them. I want to tell stories about what goes on in the minds and hearts of people who are different. Those kinds of stories might encourage people to think more, to care more about other people, and to do better.

Another thing I'd love to do is start a get-off-your-booty boot camp for people with disabilities and also for parents of the disabled. Having a disability doesn't mean you can't do any physical activity—even though I have

CP, I love going to spin class! My idea is for a two-week camp with lots of exercise and healthful food that would show people how much more energetic you feel when you're in great shape.

So sometimes I wonder if the reason I haven't found an educated, loving man is because being in a relationship would get in the way of reaching these dreams. I don't know, of course, but that's the great thing about believing everything happens for a reason. If I didn't believe that, I might be a little depressed right now, but I do believe it, so I'm okay and hopeful.

I refuse to let anyone get me down. For instance, when I was in high school a boy signed my yearbook by writing, "I always had a good time making fun of you." This was a boy who laughed at my clothes, laughed at me for wearing makeup, and was always saying I was stupid. Well, for one thing, I'm not stupid. And for another, his kind of cruelty makes no sense to me at all. I've cried over meanness like that, and even sobbed—but never for long. Sure, I can sit and cry, but then ten minutes later I get up, dry my eyes, wash my face, and go on. Because the great thing about having a disability is that it makes you a fighter; it makes you appreciate everything you have; it makes you bust your bum for what you want. Everyone's life has hardships. We all have unanswered prayers and moments of heartache and pure sadness. I've always wished it was possible to bypass those things, but the older I get, the more I see that no one ever does.

Being me hasn't been easy. All through grammar school and high school I would pray every night to God to ease the pain, the embarrassment, the sadness. In fact, I prayed all the time and I still do. Even now, every time I walk, move, or have to do something, I am praying. I always hope He will hear me, and sometimes I think He does.

When I pray, I always start out with the kind of praise and gratitude I learned in church: I say, "Dear Lord, you are almighty, all knowing, and all powerful. Thank you so much for all the blessings you have given me." Then I would ask, "Please, dear Lord, help me walk into class today and not fall. Please hold on to my arm and don't let anyone notice I walk different."

It was a huge heartache when God didn't answer my prayers. But then I guess He knows more than I do, because if He had answered those prayers, I would never have found my backbone and inner strength.

What I do know is that life goes on. And it's the times in your life when you feel saddest that you have to get up and figure out what you're going to do to fix it. Bad times have a way of making the good times seem even better. So while it's true that living my life can be difficult, it's definitely doable, as long as I face my problems and deal with them one by one. For instance, I love doing things alone, but it's really hard—as in, almost impossible—for me to do something as simple as walk through a mall without some form of help. I solved that one by keeping a baby stroller in the trunk of my car. When I get to the mall I take it out and lean on it as I go from store to store, and it makes my walking so much easier. What I found out is that people give you that pitying stare if you use a walker, but most of the time they'll smile at you if you're pushing a stroller. Sometimes people look into the stroller and probably wonder where the baby is, but thankfully, they never ask!

People tell me that my story is unique, and to tell you the truth, I know it is. But I also know that, in a lot of ways, I'm as typically small-town American as you can get. For one thing, I grew up on a pig farm in Kewanee, Illinois, where the population is about 12,000 and where one of the events that's a really big deal is the annual Hog Days festival. Then there's the fact that two of the people who've inspired me most are both self-made and came from nothing. Mary Kay Ash, the business tycoon, was a woman who really lived the American dream, starting a company of her own that became supersuccessful and—to this day—gives so many women opportunities to do well in the business world. Another big inspiration is Walt Disney, who said one of my very favorite things: "All our dreams can come true if you have the courage to pursue them."

We all have dreams, wishes, and wants, but we hide them. We keep them to ourselves because maybe someone will make fun of our dreams, or maybe we will fail. But the bottom line is that we all wake up in the morning and get out of bed each day, because somehow, no matter what other people say or think about us, we believe in our dreams.

Nobody wants to be pitied. What I've always wanted is to walk into a room and have people say, "Wow, I'm so glad you're here!" Like anyone, I want to be accepted, to be the person in the family everyone admires, the person all my relatives hope will show up on the holidays. My goal has always been to stand out—not because I don't walk like most people, but because I have dreams and achieve them.

Of course there are times when I've doubted myself, especially when I was entering beauty pageants and absolutely no one thought I should. I'd get really scared and think, *No one with a disability has ever done this before.* But then I'd tell myself, *Someone has to make the impossible possible. Maybe it can be me. Why not?*

ONE
Life on the Farm

Growing up a hog farmer's daughter, my early childhood was spent in the most rural part of Kewanee, Illinois, where there are dirt roads and no stoplights, where people call themselves cowboys and have horses and farms and drive pickups instead of cars. In the country, everyone waves at everyone, even if they don't know you. My heart will always be in the country, but at some point I realized there's a whole big wonderful world out there and I wanted a piece of it!

When I was very young, I thought it would be so cool to live in town, where there were sidewalks and a Dairy Queen, plus a whole bunch of other places: a giant Walmart, a Pizza Hut, a bank, a dentist, a doctor, a farm store, and Cerno's Bar & Grill.

But looking back, I'm grateful for my deep country roots, because living on a farm, you see and experience so much beauty: shooting stars, rainbows, pure silence, the smell of blooming flowers, coyotes running across the fields. When you live in the country, you learn to play by yourself and not be bored. You aren't afraid of the dark or of any animal—except maybe the really big ones. You know it's okay to eat veggies right out of the garden, and you know you can chew on weeds because you watch your dad do it. You pick ears of corn out of the field and husk them and eat them right then and there.

When you're a country girl, you own a few pairs of cowboy boots and one of them is your good pair. You know what sows and mares and foals and colts are. You know that duct tape fixes everything and that with a little wire and twine and a bit of paint you can create the most beautiful artistic masterpieces. You play in the mud, and you get to go to the machine shed, where farmhands dump the corn kernels and form them into giant piles ten feet high. It's a lot of fun trying to climb those piles of corn, even though you always sink into them and get really dirty.

A few years ago, my friends and I had a bonfire out on my dad's farm, and when the coyotes came pretty close and howled, my friends—who had never lived on a farm—jumped up and ran away screaming. But being a farm girl, I knew the coyotes wouldn't eat us; they would just run away.

The house I grew up in for the first years of my life was an old Victorian farmhouse. It was gray with white trim and had two big porches, one in the front and one in the back. When you pulled into the gravel drive, you'd see dozens of pigs on your left. You'd also see a big turkey and some quacking geese and a collie named Do Dah, who was so sweet but so big that I was always afraid she would knock me over. Anytime she would come running toward me, I'd anchor myself by holding on tight to my father's hand or to a chair or a tree or whatever was nearby. My parents were sure I had nothing to fear from Do Dah. And they were right, because she and I became great friends. She taught me that a big animal can also be very gentle.

If you were at my house, right away what would hit you are the sounds and the smell of the pigs. Those sounds are unique; they're little oinks and grunts and the occasional squeal. Every night I fell asleep to the distant howl of coyotes and the noise of the pigs opening and closing their food bins. I loved the crisp sound of tin hitting tin as the feeder lids slammed shut.

The smells are a different story. As a child on the farm, I woke up every day to a "fine perfume" also known as pig poop. But I never minded it, and anytime I smell animal manure—no matter where I happen to be—I feel comfortable, like I'm home.

It probably seems pretty weird to you that pig poop says "home" to me, and, in fact, there are lots of other scents on a farm that are also homey and more fragrant: there's sweet honeysuckle and wheat, and fresh-cut grass and the deep scent of lilacs. Those are soothing smells, and they make life on a farm feel so peaceful.

Beyond our house, you'd see the garage where I kept a rabbit named Piglet, and just beyond that, you'd see the huge red machine shed where my pony, Crackers, was tied. Behind the shed, you'd see lots of John Deere tractors, and then the barn where there were straw bales stacked all the way to the ceiling. We also used the barn to store at least one plow, extra wood, and a mower, and my beautiful black-and-white cat, Molly, lived there with all of her baby kittens, hiding in the straw. Past the barn, there's a big yard where I had an awesome play set. My parents had dug a big, wide hole in the ground and filled it in with mesh and wood chips and then put in a playhouse, a sandbox, a slide, swings, and a jungle gym. It was pretty cool.

You'd for sure run into my grandpa Gene, who was my dad's dad. My dad called him Rammy, because he was always ready to ram his way through any situation. For instance, Dad would get a new lawnmower and Grandpa Gene wouldn't know how to use it—and he refused to read the instructions—but that wouldn't stop him from taking off with it until he rammed it into a ditch. He was just a total get-up-and-go kind of guy. Some days after school or on weekends, or during summer afternoons, I'd ride in the truck with Dad to help with chores. On a farm, there's always work to do, like planting or picking corn or beans or checking on the sows or fixing a fence or feeding the pigs their usual fare of corn and soybean meal mixed with minerals and vitamins. From the time I was about six years old, I sometimes played a joke on my dad. When he'd get out of the truck to feed the animals, I'd wait until he got to the middle of a big bunch of hogs and then I'd reach over and hold down the horn. The sound made the pigs run away so fast the dirt and dust would be flying everywhere and you couldn't even see Dad anymore. He'd come back mad and say, "Why would you do that?" I would say, "Because it's superfunny!"

Of course, growing up on a hog farm has some strange aspects. Not every child is lucky enough to glance out the window over their bowl of Froot Loops to see Rendering Works pull in. Rendering Works are the dead-animal-disposal men who would come to my house if we needed them to pick up a dead pig or two. I never got up close and personal with the disposal men, but I could recognize them because they always seemed to be tall, stocky men dressed in bright plaid shirts and bib overalls. They would arrive in a big red open truck and you could see dead cows' feet sticking out over the top. I don't recommend it for digestion.

I was two years old when I was diagnosed with cerebral palsy. Although I was born with CP, it was so localized and mild that no one knew there was any sort of problem until I started walking—or, to be really accurate about it, when I *tried* to walk. That was when we discovered that my left leg was nearly useless, causing me to limp as I dragged it behind me.

So when I was two, both of my legs were put into ugly plastic braces that had thick brown Velcro straps. What I remember most about that time in my life was that I was crawling around on the floor at family get-togethers when my cousins who were the same age as me were already walking. I crawled a lot. Sometimes the Velcro stuck to the carpet and I would get caught and couldn't move at all. I would have to wait for someone to come and free me, and I would lie there crying until they did. But it didn't stop me from crawling. Even when I was six years old, I would still crawl. I've seen videos of myself doing that at our family's Christmas parties. All the adults would be looking at me with these alarmed expressions on their faces, but I looked completely happy. I was a very fast crawler. And I liked crawling. The other thing I really liked to do was slide down the stairs on my butt. Walking down them was really hard for me and I would be afraid I might fall, but sliding down those stairs was fun.

My girl cousins would come to my grandma's house for holiday dinners, and the strange thing was that instead of thinking I was pitiful or stupid or something, they actually envied me.

They would say, "I want your leg braces," and I would say, "You can have them." So I'd take them off and they'd strap them on and walk around in them—they thought they were cool. But that didn't make me feel any better about wearing the braces. Frankly, I would have been more than happy to give them away! I tried to do that a lot, but of course my parents would say I had to keep them, and soon they'd be back on my legs again. Still, that was a pretty good time in my life. I knew I was different back then, but it didn't matter yet.

By the time I got to preschool, it wasn't just my limp that made me stand out. Just as bad was that my feet smelled horrible because they were in hot plastic braces all day. I was embarrassed about that from a very early age.

One of my escapes when I was little was to watch Disney films like *Cinderella*. I loved that one because it's so magical to see her turn into a beautiful princess. Another movie I watched a lot was *101 Dalmatians*, because I loved the main character Cruella de Vil, with her fancy car and long fake fingernails, and the bunch of puppies. I also have always loved SpongeBob SquarePants because he's just a happy little nerd, so uncool that he's cool. But what I loved watching most of all was *The Little Mermaid*, because I could really identify with what Ariel sings about: how she wants to walk and run and be part of the world.

I've sung that song to myself a thousand times, and I don't think anyone could ever understand what it means to me. When you're a disabled kid, you have to face the fact that no one understands how you feel. No one could ever know how badly you want to do something simple like skip down the street or ride a bike—a real bike. When I was really young, I could ride a bike as long as it had training wheels. You see, my legs work fine on a bike, but because of the CP, I have no sense of balance, and the training wheels solved that problem. So I rode a training bike until about fourth grade, when everyone else I knew was already riding a regular bike. I still needed those training wheels, so I stopped riding altogether because I didn't want people to make fun of me.

What made me the loneliest back then was that no one could grasp how badly I hated my walk. In fact, I still hate it. Even today, if I had one wish, it would be to walk like other people. Just like the Little Mermaid, I want to run around. I want to run a race and play volleyball. I want to wear supertall, cute wedges and go everywhere in them and walk fast and not worry about falling on my face or breaking my ankles.

I want to walk through a room full of strangers and not have them stare. They stare like they're thinking, *What is wrong with her?* and I just want to say, "Hey, I am well aware of my 'problem.' I ask God every single day what is wrong with me." But of course I can't say those things out loud. Sometimes I've felt really sad about my situation, but I've always been aware that my family feels even worse. Whenever I've mentioned anything about CP to my parents, my dad is silent. Basically, he doesn't acknowledge that I have it. He doesn't make any allowances for it, and you might think I would resent him for that, but I don't. As far as I can see, the way my dad has always treated me is probably the main reason I learned to be independent. He expected me to do the things any kid would do, like when he wanted me to put my kittens in the barn at night—which meant I had to carry them there from my playhouse or the flower beds or wherever they were outside. Obviously, with an armful of kittens, I could fall facedown on the gravel, but that didn't keep him from insisting that I do it. He was tough, and sometimes his attitude upset me, but I also know it made me strong.

One great thing about my dad is that he would play with me every day. From the time I was a toddler until I was in middle school, we'd play a game we made up ourselves called Wild Bull. The bull was meant to be one of those mean bulls in Spain. My dad would get down on his knees and play the bull, and I played the farmer who had to feed him. So I would crawl from the kitchen to the living room with the "food," which would actually be one of my dolls, and I would have to put the food in front of the bull and then hurry away to my princess tent. I loved this game. I was really scared by the "bull," but I loved it anyway.

As for my mother: Well, she's a crier. So when I was

a kid, even if I said something really mild like, "I wish I could jump rope" and said it just in a casual way, she would start crying and saying, "I'm sorry . . . I did everything right when I was pregnant with you: I didn't drink, didn't smoke, didn't do anything I wasn't supposed to do, didn't even have a soda. I have no idea what happened."

I know my having CP is not her fault, and I don't like to make her feel bad, so I try not to bring it up. There have been times when I would have liked to talk with my parents about CP. But actually, not being able to do so turned out to be another one of those things that seem bad but was good—because it taught me to suck it up and deal with it. Life goes on. Things could be a whole lot worse. I could have cancer, I could be homeless and starving, I could be falling asleep to the sound of screams and gunshots, but I am not. I am fine, besides walking a little different and falling down sometimes. For me, like for a lot of people, the question has always been: Are you going to sit home and cry about it, or are you going to get up and try to be the best person you can be? I choose the latter.

One thing I had to realize is that hearing anything about CP makes most of the people I know feel bad, too. So I decided long ago that I can't expect them to help me with problems I have because of my disability, and that

I need to handle them by myself. When I was younger and dealing with my feelings on my own, I felt a little bit of sadness, but I always shared what I felt with my cat, Molly, and my pony, Crackers. And now that I am older, I don't bawl and tell the whole story about "poor me, why me." But luckily I do have a few great friends— I can tell them just about everything and they usually make me feel great. I have one best friend from college and another best friend in Kewanee, and I still work my butt off to make more friends. But I would rather have just a few totally amazing, true friends than a ton of fake, fair-weather friends.

In grade school, although I was friendly with a lot of kids, my very best friends were the animals on the farm. Because of them, I felt like I had many friends. They loved me for who I was and never made fun of me or thought I was different. I got my cat, Molly, when I was four, on the day we took our dog Do Dah to get her shots at the vet. There was a cat there who didn't have a home. She was a fluffy black-and-white cat with the prettiest big eyes. The minute I saw her, I fell in love. My mom let me bring her home, and from the very first day, Molly and I were inseparable! Since I was an only child, living way out in the country far from other kids, Molly was so important to me. We would have lunch in my Little Tykes playhouse or drive around in my Barbie car, and I'd talk to her for hours. Before long, she gave birth to kittens, and that was wonderful, since it meant more best friends for me.

Over the years, Molly had many litters of kittens. On Sundays, my grandma Wink—my mother's mother—would get a large laundry basket and we would load up all of Molly's kittens. We'd take them to visit Great-Grandma Bootsie, who was ninety-nine years old and lived out in an old farmhouse. That poor old woman—she didn't have any toys, and she was so old and had one leg amputated, but the kitties made her happy—I'd set them all out and they'd crawl all over her and burrow in her skirts and arms.

Since I was an only child, I lucked out by being the only grandchild on my mom's side of the family. That meant I saw my grandma Wink and my grandpa Jack every single day. I spent most of my childhood with them because my dad farmed and worked the hogs every day and Mom is a nurse who worked three twelve-hour shifts every week at a huge hospital an hour away from our house. Of course, Grandma Wink and Grandpa Jack worked, too. Grandpa Jack was the postmaster at his local post office, and Grandma is a nurse. The four of them arranged their schedules so

I never had to go to a babysitter or day care. On the days Mom and Dad worked, Mom would drive me to my grandparents' house. I always looked forward to those afternoons when my grandparents watched me. Grandpa Jack and I would stand outside his front door and he'd say, "Wave good-bye to Momma," and then I knew the fun would start. Anything I wanted to do, we could do. A lot of times I played doctor, and Grandpa Jack would let me glue Kleenex to his arms to look like a cast, or cover him in Band-Aids. We'd take a trip "up town" in Sheffield, where they lived, and visit the tax office of my uncle John, who is an accountant. Then we'd go to the post office and say hello to Grandpa's friends, then to the grocery store, not to buy anything but to say hello to more friends, like the guy who worked at the meat counter.

Afterward, we'd make our way up to the gas station, where I was allowed to buy any and every candy I wanted, like Ring Pops in the shape of diamonds and those little wax bottles you bite the top off of and then drink the sweet liquid inside them.

The doctor's office where my grandma Wink worked was right across the street from the gas station, so after I'd eaten every bit of my candy, I'd go back there to be with her. I loved to visit her there because I would always get to "help." I got to print labels for the urine specimen cups that I called pee cups; I'd get to sort the ink pens the drug reps gave away for free; and I'd get to press a button or two and say hello to the doctor or nurse practitioner. I felt pretty cool doing all that. I hadn't yet realized that someday, when I was all grown up, I would want to become a nurse like both of my grandmas and my mother. When I was little, I had other ideas—I was busy most of the day being a cowgirl, which basically meant riding and grooming my horse. If you had asked me back then what I was going to do when I grew up, I'd have told you I was going to be a cowgirl. I didn't realize that it wasn't an actual job.

On the days Grandma Wink wasn't working, she'd come to my house and crazy things would happen. All of a sudden, Molly and her kittens were allowed in and all over the house. So were the dog and the turkey. When my parents were home, the animals were never allowed to come indoors and play, so this was very exciting. We would dress the kittens in baby doll clothes and play house with them. When Grandma Wink came over, she was always up to something: planting flowers or washing windows or bringing a meat grinder and grinding up some turkey or chicken for a salad or making homemade ice cream. Sometimes, she'd make freezer corn, which you make by boiling ears of corn, cutting the corn off the cob, putting it into Ziploc bags, and freezing them so in the middle of winter you can pull one out, stick it in the microwave, and enjoy yummy sweet summer corn. When I hung out with my grandparents, starting from the time I was really little until I was in fifth or sixth grade, we'd go back to their house and Grandma would help me with my homework. Because we both liked to play, we'd get through it really fast. Then, she'd play piano and I'd dress up and dance around the room (yes—I can dance) and we'd both sing. Or we'd play church and baptize all my baby dolls. We'd play Chinese checkers, or we'd go outside and take walks around the farm, or play with sidewalk chalk; we'd catch lightning bugs and collect them in a jar that always had a thin little stick in it for them to rest on and a couple of holes in the lid so they could breathe. I love lightning bugs. They are magical and they don't even know it, which makes me love them even more. Another game Grandma Wink and I would play is hide-and-seek, or we'd go way out into the fields and pick wildflowers until we had baskets filled with little tiny white and yellow and purple blossoms.

I had so much fun with Grandma Wink. The woman seriously cannot sit still. I don't think I have ever watched a movie or a TV show with her because she'll always say,

"We need to be doing something."

If you said, "One of these days, I really need to paint my house," she'd jump up and say, "Okay, let's get it done," and within an hour, she'd have gone to the store to buy paint and then come back and started painting. The only times she would stop moving all around was when it was really cold or rainy and we had to stay indoors. Then we'd sit by the fire and she'd read to me. But pretty soon she'd be up doing loads of laundry or cleaning the house from top to bottom.

We'd mess around all day and then Grandma Wink would cook dinner. Usually, my mom wasn't home because she's a nurse in a hospital, which meant she was gone fourteen hours most days. So once it started getting dark, my dad would come in from farming and Grandpa Jack would drive over and sometimes Uncle John would come, too, and Grandma Wink and I would "meet the guys for supper," which was always good, basic food like meat loaf with mashed potatoes, or chicken croquettes with white sauce and peas, or ham steaks with baked beans and brown bread. The best nights were Wednesday nights, when we'd go to a small town a few miles away called Neponset and get Henny Pennys, which is a really delicious dish of fried chicken, french fries, and coleslaw. Afterward, we'd go home and watch reruns of *Lawrence Welk*.

I will never forget those songs: "Getting to Know You" and "Shall We Dance" from *The King and I*, and "You Make Me Feel So Young," and always the *Lawrence Welk* theme song that ended "Good night, sleep tight, and pleasant dreams to you. Here's a wish and a prayer that every dream comes true . . ."

Grandpa Jack would look at the ladies dancing and singing on TV and say, "Aren't they pretty, Abbey?"

When the show ended, Grandma Wink would head over to the piano and play songs like "Bell-Bottomed Trousers" and the Notre Dame Victory March. I'm not sure why, but I would always run to the living room and jump up in the window seat (I can and still do run and jump; it just looks a lot different from how others do it). And then I'd dance and sing as Gran played, and we'd put on a show for "the boys." My dad and my uncle and Grandpa Jack would clap and cheer, and if you listened to Grandpa Jack, you'd think I was the next LeAnn Rimes.

When my grandparents left to go home, I would open my big bedroom window and turn on the flashlight I kept beside it. I would flash it on and off, and when they saw it, they would flash their headlights back at me and turn on the lights inside the car so I could see them.

They'd be waving and honking the horn as they drove away. I don't know why we came up with this ritual, but we did it every night they came over.

On days when both of my parents worked, Grandma Wink and Grandpa Jack would pick me up at school. We would go directly to the Dairy Queen, and Grandpa would get a vanilla shake and I would get a cherry sundae. Then we'd go off to Walmart so Gran could get groceries, and Grandpa would pull out his wallet and say to Grandma, "You get that little girl anything she wants."

So I'd get a sparkle pen or a fuzzy troll or even goldfish in a giant tank. Or we'd go to the farm store next to Walmart, where one time my grandparents bought me a white bunny that I named Blackie. I love bunnies. I probably had about twenty bunnies when I was growing up; each time I'd give one away to someone else who wanted a bunny and then I would go and get more. My parents didn't mind how many animals I had. My dad's farm was on eighty acres of land, and a couple of extra bunnies or a bunch of cats barely made a difference.

A lot of nights we'd go somewhere like Andris Waunee Farm, where there were dozens of gorgeous horses and a beautiful bright red barn with white trim. It was my favorite place ever. There was a live band, a dance floor, and the biggest, most delish smorgasbord ever with the best food in the county: mashed potatoes and gravy, ribs, a carving station, Jell-O molds, lettuce with ranch dressing—my favorite—and lots of chocolate desserts.

After dinner, we'd watch the horses run, and then we'd dance to the music of the live band! It might surprise you to know that CP did not affect my dancing, at least not in my own mind.

Everyone at Waunee Farm was my friend. Okay, they were actually my grandparents' friends, but what I remember most is that no one stared, no one asked questions, no one tried to make things easier for me, and no one treated me any different while I was dancing. Most of the time, they would just pick me up and swing me around so I wasn't even dancing on the actual floor. While I was dancing at Waunee Farm, everyone was telling me how beautiful I was, how great a dancer I was, and it was all positive, so I didn't have time to remember I had cerebral palsy. I wish every girl with a disability had opportunities like this, because it really impacts your life. It makes you willing to take chances, to try to do what you want to do. It made me more confident, even though I realize everyone was probably lying to me when they said I was a good dancer. Still, it helped. I've seen girls with CP who are afraid to do anything, and if they'd had my experience, I am sure they'd take more risks and have more fun. Anyway, as far as I'm concerned, even people who don't have a disability need a giant fan club.

From the time I was four years old, my parents and grandparents took me to Disney World every year for my birthday in July. I would get all sorts of great presents: a big Minnie Mouse doll that came with its own closet filled with clothes on bright yellow hangers, and the big white Aristocat named Duchess. We would stay for ten days or two weeks, and at every meal my parents would say, "Abbey, tell them why you're here." And I would say, "For my birthday!" And we'd get free ice cream and cake at every single meal! Disney World was my absolutely favorite place to be.

Grandpa Jack wanted for me whatever I wanted for myself, so one day when I was four years old, he went off and bought me a pony. It was the greatest thing ever, because even though I had leg braces, I could ride a horse. My horse had an owner before me who had named him Crackers. It wasn't the perfect name, but it didn't matter because I loved that horse so much. He was short. Solid. He must have been about twelve hands, or fifty inches, tall. He was milk-chocolate brown with a big blond mane and tail. Like a Barbie pony. He was so totally cute, and he'd whinny when you talked to him. He was about fourteen—that's old for a horse—and very calm and slow. But to me he was a speeder, a racehorse!

I have photographs from the day I got Crackers. It must have been superwindy that day since everyone is holding on to their hats and my hair is blowing like crazy. In the photographs, I'm smiling and it looks like I must have been screaming something because I was so excited. Most girls dream of having a pony, and I actually had one! I couldn't believe he was all mine! And that meant I could be a true cowgirl—I already had the boots and the vest and the hat, but now the final piece was in place, and I was an official cowgirl!

When I was riding Crackers, I felt like I was on top of the world, and when I was allowed to ride him all by myself, with no one riding close to me, I felt like the luckiest person ever.

My grandpa Jack didn't waste any time signing me up for parades and Prettiest Pony contests. These were the best because all I had to do was ride, and I didn't have to walk or do anything that was hard for me to do because of having cerebral palsy.

I didn't think about it at the time, but looking back I can see that those contests were my opportunity to do something that was really competitive. They were one of the few things that really made me feel just like a "normal" girl. I got all excited and decked out for them. I had a special outfit with rhinestone jeans, extra-shiny cowboy boots, and a cowboy hat, and I felt so proud when Grandpa Jack led Cracker and me through the annual Sheffield Homecoming Parade.

I thought I was the coolest kid ever. I felt really great on my pony, especially since most kids I knew were just sitting on the sidelines watching the parade, eating their little bags of candy. Meanwhile, there I was, wearing my rhinestone-studded outfit and supercool hat and riding along on Crackers, who had been all fancied up by my mother and grandma, who attached big pink and purple pom-poms all through his mane and tail. It was events like this that definitely made me feel anything was possible. And anything really was possible, because the Homecoming Parade had a Best Horse or Pony contest, and Crackers and I won it! We have a photo of me sitting on Crackers and holding up a huge gold trophy and absolutely beaming! Despite the fact that it was just a prize from a hometown parade, it was one of the best days of my life. The truth is, I felt awesome just having a horse and being in the parade.

Years later, I learned that my grandpa Jack had paid the judges to let me win. When I found out, I was shocked at first, and really upset. But now, it makes me smile every time I think about it, because it shows that Grandpa Jack would have given everything he had to make me happy, and he did. How sweet is that? I know he had to pay a large sum of money, but it didn't matter to him. It made him happy to make me so happy. We took that pony trophy everywhere, and I even got my picture in the paper.

After that, thanks to Grandpa Jack, I "won" a few more pony contests. Grandpa Jack was one of a kind! He knew I didn't really have the chance to compete in anything else, and he knew that winning those pony contests meant the world to me. He was the biggest supporter I ever had. If someone said something about my leg braces or the way I walked, he would jump in and say, "You're talking about my beautiful cowgirl. She's the most beautiful girl in the world."

TWO
School Days

From kindergarten to eighth grade, I attended a small Catholic school five miles from our farmhouse. It was a private school called Visitation. Although it was Catholic, there were no nuns—but it did have the grossest hot lunch ever!

Dad took me to school every day in the big hog truck. That truck was ten times bigger than any regular-size vehicle and had squealing pigs in the back. You couldn't see the pigs unless they tried to get out, but you could hear them and smell them—so everyone knew when I arrived because the pigs in the truck were stinky and making so much noise.

If you had seen me then, you'd have seen a living mess! My mother tried to make me look better, but it was an uphill battle. Walking was so hard for me, and I ran all over all the time. That may sound strange to you, considering that I have CP. But I used to run a lot and still do. I can move really fast. I just look a lot different from other runners and I sweat a lot when I'm doing it, which isn't the most attractive thing ever. So my face would be beet red and my cowlick would be sticking right out from the side of my head. I always asked my mom why she didn't use hairspray, but my mom is just naturally pretty and isn't into girly things, so when she did my hair in the morning she'd just put it in a ponytail or put a headband on me before she rushed me out the door. So on the ride into town with Dad I'd do a little primping. All I had to do was look over at Dad, and he'd pass me the small bottle of holy water he kept in the truck and used to bless the fields. A few drops of holy water were just enough to fix my cowlick, at least for a while.

Even when I was very young I was attracted to anything or anyone that I thought was glamorous. I loved long pretty hair and high-heeled shoes and jewelry and makeup and anything that sparkled the way my rhinestone cowgirl outfit did. In first grade, I got in trouble with my teachers for carrying a pink-and-white Minnie Mouse purse that came with the cheapest, brightest kids' play makeup ever. I also wore big clip-on earrings and fake diamonds, which looked pretty funny with my starched and proper Catholic school uniform. My mother bought me the earrings and purse because I wanted them so much, but she didn't know I took them to school. She wouldn't have liked that one bit. So I would just sneak them into Dad's truck and then I was set.

There aren't a whole lot of glamorous people in Kewanee. But there was one really glamorous woman in my own family, and I adored her. This was my aunt Judy, who had a job selling Mary Kay cosmetics. Aunt Judy drove a pink Cadillac and had a little Yorkie dog. She also had bleached-blond hair and acrylic fingernails, sparkly earrings, and sparkly super-high-heeled shoes.

My grandma said she was a floozy. So I thought a floozy was someone with makeup and a little dog who gets lots of attention and probably gets an armful of Valentines from boys. By then, I was kind of over being a cowgirl, so in school, when they asked what we wanted to be when we grew up, I said, "When I grow up I want to be a floozy."

Though I wore heavy braces on my legs, I still couldn't walk without help, so from kindergarten to first grade, I supported myself on a Hello Kitty push toy. Everyone knew I needed it, and no one minded that, but it did have this one feature that always got me in trouble: As soon as I started walking, it would blare music and light up and distract other students. And it wasn't just my own class that heard it—it was every class in the entire school. Sometimes teachers would peek their heads out the door and say, "Yep, it's Abbey," and class would stop and I'd know that everyone was listening to me walk all the way down the hall toward the classroom. I hated that. Finally, I had the music box taken out of it. That was sad because the music was nice, but it was necessary.

Another thing I really hated was gym class, when we had to play dodgeball. I usually won, and that felt good at first, but then I realized that the reason I won was because no one wanted to hurl a giant ball at "the crippled girl."

I was seven and in the second grade when my doctor said I had to have surgery for heel cord lengthening, so I wouldn't walk only on my tiptoes anymore. That was the most comfortable way for me to walk, and I always thought I looked like a ballerina when I did it. I would walk way up high on my toes, but to tell you the truth, it didn't look as cool as I thought it did.

The operation isn't unusual for kids with CP. I didn't want to have it, but I didn't have a choice. For months afterward, I had to wear a huge plaster cast on each leg; the casts made my legs hot and actually weighed more than I did. One was painted purple, the other was painted pink. I guess that was supposed to make wearing them seem like fun, but there's no way that leg braces can be fun, no matter what color you make them. In the end, I still had a terrible walk, though I guess it was some sort of improvement that I didn't walk on my tiptoes anymore.

My parents divorced when I was in third grade. They stayed friends, and the situation never got ugly, thank goodness. My dad still came and picked me up for school each day, and I spent most afternoons and every weekend and holiday on the farm. Even today, I'm out there four days a week.

But when the divorce happened, I remember feeling bad for my dad because he lived out on the big farm all by himself. My mom and I only moved four miles away into a nice apartment on Midland Drive—it was a fancy area where everyone but the two of us was in their fifties, and a bunch of people were a whole lot older than that.

I remember when my mom was packing; my dad must have been working, so I got all of my stuffed animals and dolls together and put them in his bed so he wouldn't be lonely. And I wrote him dozens of notes and left them all around the house reminding him how much I loved him.

Even though my dad and I definitely fight, at the end of the day I always want to make sure he is taken care of, that he has a good dinner and freshly ironed clothes and a warm, clean house. The divorce was hard for me but, partly because I was so young, it was almost easy at the same time. I remember being sad about leaving my home, my pets, my farm. I didn't know anything about life outside the farm. The main reason the transition wasn't a big trauma is that I could go to my dad's whenever I wanted. I didn't have to miss the farm because most days my dad would get me after school and drive me out there and it was just like I had never left. So the divorce really didn't change my life too much, especially because my parents always went to my school events together and we were always together on holidays, and neither one of them ever remarried.

The hardest thing was that I couldn't stand one night without Piglet, my bunny. No pets were allowed in the apartment where my mom and I lived, but after a few lonely nights we snuck him in. That winter I remember waking up to something I had never seen before: a mouse stuck under my door. OMG! That was scary. It happened a few times. The mice were too big to move from room to room by going beneath the closed doors, but they would try to push through anyway, and it wouldn't work. Yuck. I was so scared. I'd run from my bed to my mother's room and sometimes while I was doing this they'd make a squeak that would send chills down my spine. Apparently this was all Piglet's fault, because bunnies attract mice. So that next spring I had to give Piglet to one of my dad's friends and that turned out to be the worst thing of all, because I later learned he was one of those people who eats rabbit.

When I was in fifth grade there was a lot of excitement about Botox and cerebral palsy. I remember getting called out of class so my mother could drive my best friend, Tessa, and me to the city, where I was about to get Botox injections in my legs. Tessa was the one person I wanted to have with me. She's really funny, and I thought she would be able to make me laugh even in a situation that was so totally unfunny. But neither one of us had any idea what I was in for. You hear the word *Botox* and you think it's not a big deal. Lots of celebrities get it, right? And it doesn't hurt and it's supposed to make them look younger and better. But Botox in your muscles is a whole different story. It was the worst pain I have ever felt. I remember Tessa staring at my face, trying everything to distract me. Tessa is really smart, and as she watched each single tear form and roll down my face she tried to distract me by getting all scientific and telling me about the anatomy of tears—how they're formed and where they come from. Ordinarily, that might have interested me, and I know Tessa really tried to help, but it was still a horrible experience. The doctor said, "Oh, by tomorrow you'll be showing signs of improvement." But I didn't. Not then, or ever.

The one lucky thing about those days in elementary and middle school was that the other kids didn't make fun of me. I felt safe at that school. It was the right place for me. I was in a class of about twenty kids, and I stayed with that same group until I went to high school. These kids knew me. They accepted me. If they hadn't seen me fall and limp and everything else in those nine years, then I don't know where they were. So I didn't have to worry about being stared at or being made fun of or being different. The making fun part came later, when I was older and the other kids were older, too. You would think it would be the other way around: that it would be the young kids who laughed at me because they didn't know better and the older kids would know better for sure. Instead, the older I got, the worse it got, until I came to see CP as something horrible.

THREE
A New World

The next really big change in my life happened when I went from my private Catholic school to a public high school, starting in ninth grade. For one thing, as always, I was worried about walking. Would I be able to walk into school easily, or would I have to walk through a huge parking lot? What would the hallways be like with so many more kids than I was used to? Would the kids I didn't know stare at me? Would they make fun of me? Would they like me? Would I finally be cool? Would I get to sit at the cool table? Would I get to be student council president or homecoming queen? I realize that all kids have the same kind of worries when they're starting high school, but most kids don't walk in a way that gets them all kinds of negative attention. I was always hopeful that things would work out well, but I have to say, my stomach got a little upset every time I began thinking about what high school would be like.

As it turned out, the best part about changing schools was that I didn't have to wear a uniform anymore, which was awesome—until week three, when I couldn't find anything new to wear.

Kewanee High School doesn't have air conditioning, and it's HUGE! We all know how much I love walking (yeah, right), and it was especially fun in May and June when it was superhumid and the temperature inside the school would get up to one hundred degrees.

This was a whole new world for me. I still had the same classmates I'd had since kindergarten, the kids who never made fun of me. But now I was with three hundred other students who I didn't know at all. Have you ever seen the movies *The Breakfast Club* and *Mean Girls*? Well, I assumed high school would be like both those movies put together. I thought kids would be divided into cliques like they are in *The Breakfast Club*: You have the guys who are so cool, the leather-jacket-wearing, skipping-school, motorcycle-riding guys. Then you have the cute, popular, makeup-wearing, pink-loving, sweet girls. You have the Goth girls who the cute, sweet, pink-loving girls turn into pink-loving, cute girls like them. Then you have the guys in varsity jackets, and the guys who wear knitted sweater vests and are momma's boys. So I pictured high school like that, with a splash of *Mean Girls*. In that movie, there's a group of mean girls—aka the popular ones—who rule the school and drive fancy cars, and get anything and everything they want, and are super, superpretty, and put on lip gloss as they walk down the hallways in giant heels.

But high school wasn't like that at all. For one thing, in the movies, kids skip class and go have fun. When kids skipped class in real high school, they either got detentions or suspensions.

When I started high school, my dad still drove me to school every day. By then, in addition to running the farm, he had taken a part-time job at the post office, so we drove in a regular truck—in other words, no more squealing pigs. He had also walked me to the grammar school's front door every single day, and carried my book bag and walked me to my locker, so why would that change for high school? Answer: It didn't. On the first day of school, I was in biology class when I heard one of my new classmates say, "Someone's daddy had to walk them all the way to their locker." It was a boy seated just to my left, who was one of the "coolest" guys in the school, even though now those guys don't work much and never went to college, which shows you how much being "cool" can be worth. When he said it, I kind of cried. Not full-out crying, but I was upset. I am just a crier like my mother, darn it—I cry when I am happy; I cry when I am sad; I cry when I am angry and when I am scared. And on that day, it made me so mad that someone would have the nerve to comment on my dad helping me when what were they doing? Watching me? Laughing at me? Why didn't they ask if they could help? I would have! So I said, "Yes, my dad helps me, and he does it because no one else helps me. No one else holds my arm or carries my bag or walks me to class."

I mean, did I want my dad to have to help me? No. I didn't want to need any help at all. But I *did* need help, and when I heard those jerks laughing at me, I wanted to smack them. What kinds of parents raise kids like that? I was taught that if you can't say something nice, you don't say anything at all.

Now that I was in a new school, I discovered that another good thing about having CP (again, kidding) was that I never had to worry about teachers remembering my name. I wasn't Samantha who had the great smile or Jane who had the pretty blond hair or Susan who was supertall and thin. I was the only "disabled" person in the class, so remembering the name Abbey was easy. But basically the first few weeks of high school were bad news: trying to get my locker open between classes, carrying huge books, and having only minutes to get through crowded hallways. By the time each school day ended, I was a hot mess. I looked awful, but I'd like to think we all have bad days. Even the so-called normal people don't feel awesome about themselves every day. So you have to accept that you can't be anywhere close to perfect all the time—if ever. And you have to learn to think on the bright side. You have to give yourself things to work toward and look forward to.

One thing I saw in high school was that kids worry so much about being cool. For them, that's what it's about. For me, no matter what I did or didn't do, I was never going to be cool or be a popular kid, that's for sure. So I thought, *Okay, I can't be cool, but I can be nice.*

Another thing that made high school especially scary was that I was coming from Catholic school, where everyone had worn a uniform and gone to church. There were so many people I wasn't used to at the high school, like people who said "F U" and girls who fought in the hallway— mean girls pulling each other's hair—and I would just think, *Oh my God, I don't want to be here.* But then the next day, I'd see one of the girls who was pulling some-one's hair do something really nice for somebody and I'd realize that people have more than one side to them, and that I had to accept that most people can be kind as well as cruel. Knowing that helped me to not be so afraid of people. For instance, there were guys with tattoos who smoked and had gauges in their ears who I would nor-mally be afraid of, but they turned out to be really nice guys. They weren't the ones who were making fun of me walking down the hallway. The ones who made fun of me were the preppy kids who thought they were better than everyone else.

During my sophomore year, I pulled a groin muscle. I went to the hospital and had X-rays, but they said there was nothing I could do but try to rest it. Since a girl with CP can't balance, crutches were out. The pain in my groin was so horrible I couldn't walk. But I made myself walk anyway. I didn't want to look like a help-less invalid, so I refused to use a wheelchair. I walked even though a lot of times my leg would give out and I'd drop to the ground, and I wasn't getting anywhere, so I'd have to take a moment to rest. To me, it shows that no matter what I need to do, I can do it without anyone's help; it shows that I am not going to stop life because of a challenge. I figure out how to fix it and I make it work. Sometimes it takes a day to figure out a good solution, but I always do. Sure, it would be nice at times to have help, and I've had moments when I want help, but that's different than needing it. I am 110 percent independent. Just tell me I can't do something and I will prove you wrong, I promise.

After a while, I did make some new friends, though I never felt I was a good friend because I always needed them to hold on to, and I mean that literally. They would let me do it because they were amazing, but, for example, a normal activity like going shopping wasn't a fun girl time. I would get all hot and sweaty; walking down long hallways was hard, and I would have to lean on their arms all day. I made them hot, I made their arms sore. I felt horrible! I was "work" for them. And I didn't want to embarrass them. I know people stare at me, but I don't like my friends to see that. I would never want anyone to feel sorry for me.

FOUR
Pageant Girl

s far back as I can remember, I had gone to the local beauty pageant—the Miss Henry County contest—which is held at the fairgrounds on a stage built smack in the middle of a racetrack for cars.

I still go, always with my mother and my grandma Wink, who love the pageant as much as I do. We'd be so excited to get there, and we would show up as early as possible so we could sit in the middle of the second row. They hand out programs with pictures of all the girls and each of us would pick who we thought the top five would be and try to list them in the right order. Then we'd bet among ourselves on who would be the winner.

I really admired every one of the contestants. They were all confident young women, usually about forty of them, who ranged in age from sixteen to twenty-one and who weren't scared to speak their minds, share their hearts, and strut their stuff in front of the huge crowds of people judging them. Not a lot of people can say they'd be able to do that.

It's funny: I know people who act all high and mighty sitting at a lunch table, but let's see how confident they are in front of such a big audience, with spotlights on them and a microphone to make sure everyone hears what they have to say. I think even some of the most popular kids would be a mess, rambling words, crying, running offstage. We "losers" have learned that we all mess up and we all make mistakes, and the only way to handle a situation like that is to not give up and run away but to smile and stay there and do your best. That's one of the many things I learned from being in pageants. Another thing I learned is that it's better to put yourself out there and take a chance than to sit home and do nothing.

The fairgrounds always had all sorts of things going on. There were flashing lights and carnival games and the screams of people on a big roller coaster called the Star Trooper. I always wanted to go on the Star Trooper, but I am not too great with motion, so I always chicken out. But I loved being at the fair, especially going to where the beautiful show horses were on display. It always made me happy to be around horses, even if they weren't mine. After Grandpa Jack bought me Crackers, my first pony, I was lucky enough that he bought me a few others, just because he knew I loved them. By the time I was in high school, my ponies had passed on, since they were already really old when I got them, but the ponies at the fair brought back all kinds of wonderful memories . . . And of course, the smell of animal manure coming from the barns reminded me of home.

I loved the food smells, too, from the good ol' fair food: popcorn, cotton candy, taffy, elephant ears, ice cream, onion rings, turkey legs, nachos, deep-fried pickles on a stick, and two of my favorites, giant corn dogs and funnel cakes. For taste, you can't beat them.

My absolute favorite moment of the fair was when the announcer said, "Welcome to the Miss Henry County Fair Queen Pageant." It gave me goose bumps. Another thing I loved was getting dressed up for the fair. I remember being little and wearing a bright pink sundress with a big front pocket. I still go to the Miss Henry County pageant and still get dressed up for it. This year, I wore a fitted navy-and-white-striped top with a big navy bow around the waist, dark jeans with some rhinestones on them, taupe wedges, and rhinestone hoop earrings. Back when I was in my early teens and even before that, my goal in getting dressed up for the pageant was for someone in the grandstands to tell me I was so pretty I should be in the pageant myself. But unfortunately, it never happened.

From the time I was three years old, I dreamed of entering that contest. My family would all say, "Yes, you can do it," and they kept saying that until I was about twelve. But the older I got, the less we talked about it, because I was shy and scared. I'd tell my mom I was going to enter the contest and she would say, "Okay, but once you enter, you can't drop out."

She knows me too well. I would have rather had her say, "Oh, yay! We have to go dress shopping!" but she knew I was a chicken—so I guess the reason she'd say it was okay for me to enter was because she thought I never would. Actually, I had never chickened out of anything with the one exception of Girl Scouts. I decided to leave Girl Scouts after a lot of the girls laughed at me because I moved slower than they did and in such a herky-jerky way. After I quit, my mother started telling me that once I said I would do something, I had to keep my word and do it.

The one and only person who actually believed I

could be a "beauty queen" was my grandpa Jack. Even when I was really little, he would tell me that someday I'd be Miss America! As you can see, he was just an amazing guy who never doubted me. He was selfless. His girls always came first: my grandma Wink, my mom, whose name is Katie, and me. We were his world, and there was one way I knew that for sure: His second loves, after the three of us, were his racehorses, and he named them Wink's Pride, Good Katie, and Abbey Curran.

Grandpa Jack thought I was the most beautiful, greatest, smartest, most talented person ever! I don't know why, but he did.

But by the time I got to high school, I assumed I'd never do a pageant. I was the challenged girl, the one who limped, the one who had never been on a date, never been kissed, never went to a party, never been chosen first, never had clear skin, never had anything anyone else wanted. I was the one who wasn't glamorous, so why would I be in a pageant? And you know how much I hated my clumsy walk. I didn't want to parade around and show that walk to the world. Still, I couldn't help but be attracted to pageants, because entering one would be such a different thing for a girl with a physical disability to do. Disabled girls are like anyone else: We also want to be looked at as poised and desirable and beautiful, even though I didn't believe I was any of those things.

In Kewanee, the Miss Henry County Fair pageant is a really big deal. The girls who sign up for it are head of the cheerleading squad, the homecoming queen, the winner of the state track competition, the choreographer of the pom-pom squad. They are the gorgeous girls, the popular girls, the successful girls who are on local radio every week and have their pictures in the newspapers because they're heading up a blood bank drive or working at a pancake breakfast to benefit the fire department, or were just elected class president or Athlete of the Week.

Everyone wants to be best friends with them. I was sort of friends with the ones who went to my school, but I wasn't at their level, which made me sad. Basically, I had two good friends—one was my best friend, Tessa, who went with me when I had the Botox injection and had been my friend since first grade. Back then, we both liked to play with dolls, and when we got older, we both loved to go to the Sale Barn. We'd go and look at all the animals and pet them and then we'd go to my house and order a sausage pizza and watch movies. Tessa lived in public housing and never invited me over, I think because she was embarrassed about it, though I always told her there was no reason for her to feel that way.

My other friend was Sam, whose real name is Samantha and who sat at the popular girls' table. I would have liked to hang out with the cool girls, the A students, the athletes. But I was different. I didn't read books all the time like the straight-A students, and even if I didn't have cerebral palsy, I doubt I would be a star athlete running at top speeds, leaping hurdles gracefully like a deer, or doing backflips across the basketball court at halftime. Still, I looked up to these girls. I was always hoping to be invited to their parties.

One of the popular girls became my barometer. Her name was Rachel, and she was five-foot-eleven, with long, straight blond hair. She was a big track star, a champion who won hundred-meter dashes and long jump contests, and because of that, her picture was plastered all over the interstate signs.

Rachel was the Miss America of our school. She was also class president. She was the one person in the elite, supercool group willing to be friends with me. She wasn't like the other girls who would talk about "fun" activities they had done with their boyfriends over the weekend and then I would walk in the bathroom and they would stop talking about it and say, "You wouldn't understand, Abbey."

That would make me so mad! Even worse was that they made fun of me all the time. They'd say my clothes were baby clothes because they were from a store for tweens, but it sold the kind of clothes I love—things like T-shirts covered in rhinestones or sequins or glitter.

I drove an old Mary Kay Cosmetics car that had advertisements for Mary Kay makeup plastered all over it. The car had been a prize to my aunt Judy, who won it by selling lots of Mary Kay products. I was so happy to have that car. But if any of my classmates saw me pull into school with it, I would hear about it all day. Kids made so much fun of me that my mother said, "Don't drive it to school, keep it home and keep it safe."

But I wanted to drive it, so I got stubborn about it and drove it to school every single day. I loved that car, and I thought then, as I do now, that it is stupid to hide who I am because some shallow kids don't like the same things I do.

Rachel was one of the only people who didn't tease me about the car. I appreciated that she could look beyond my CP. She was so cool that she didn't care what anyone else thought, and I guess that's why she wasn't embarrassed to be my friend. When Rachel said she was entering the Miss Henry County contest, everyone said it was wonderful. I knew if I entered, everyone would say it was a joke. I thought, *Why is it a joke? Why can't I be as good as anyone else?*

So, just after I turned sixteen, I began to think seriously about entering the pageant and having the courage to compete against Rachel. There comes a time when you need to dare to do something even if you're totally scared to do it. Bottom line: my dream was to be a beauty queen. And the only thing stopping me from trying was the opinions of people I didn't want to care about anyway.

I sat down and made a list of the pros and the cons. Pros: I could win the contest, I could feel pretty, I could buy a beautiful dress, I could make new friends. Cons: I could lose, and people would make fun of me and talk about how uncool I was. But since people already made fun of me, that wouldn't be anything new, and I already wasn't cool, so that wouldn't be new, either. When I really looked at the situation it was clear that I had a lot more pros than cons. So I thought, *What the heck? Why not?*

Of course, everyone I knew—my friends, my family, the cool people, guys at school—did everything they could to discourage me from entering the contest. Even my favorite teacher at the time said, "Oh, Abbey, be realistic. You can't do that." The day she said I couldn't do it, I sent away for the entry papers.

I didn't know anything about being in a pageant. One of the first things I did was pick out a dress my mother liked. Now that my mother hadn't been able to talk me out of it, she did whatever she could to help me do well in the pageant. We went to a dress shop just across the state line in Bettendorf, Iowa, called My Lady Boutique, and it was perfect! It was run by the kindest woman, named Brenda, who was so helpful. She continued to be in my pageant life, finding beautiful gowns for me whenever I needed one for a local competition. The gown I picked out for Miss Henry County was white and strapless, with splashes of hot pink and pastel pink sequins. Because it was strapless and because I walk with a little twist and kind of side to side, I was really worried it might fall down. But the seamstress fit the dress to the shape of my body and kept making it tighter. She said, "The rib cage is so tight, this dress isn't going anywhere."

That first pageant was quite the experience. The day it was going to be held, I was sick and weak and when I opened my eyes it was like watching snow on the TV. I was that nervous. I couldn't see, which meant I was close to passing out. Part of me wanted to back out of the pageant; the rest of me wanted to do it just so I could get it over with. Because I knew that if I didn't compete in the pageant, I'd wonder for the rest of my life, *What if . . . how different would my life be if I had just gone ahead and been in that contest?*

Anyway, my mom saw me sitting on the porch and said it didn't matter how bad I felt. She said, "You gave your word you would be in this competition; you don't back down on your word."

So, like I do with many things in my life, I had to suck it up. I knew that the only choices I had were to worry and make myself sick or to pull myself together and talk myself out of being so worried. So I said to myself, *It's going to be fine, it's just a pageant, it's just for fun.*

I talk to myself like this a lot. And it was really important at that moment because I somehow knew that if I wasn't able to do this pageant, I would never pull myself together and never leave my house, never go to college, never have a life.

Sure, life is scary. Life can make you feel sick, afraid, anxious, but when you go out and do something you want to do, it's worth every heart-pounding, blood-rushing, can't-catch-your-breath moment. Today, one of the things I am proud of myself for is that if I say I am going to do something, I do it. It doesn't matter how nerve-racking it seems, because the feeling afterward is priceless! At the Miss Henry County Fair pageant, I had a point to prove. The point was that a person with a disability can compete like anyone else.

The grandstands for the pageant were packed full, and I was so excited and nervous. But even though I'm nervous a lot of the time, I always try my best to fool everybody and never let them realize it.

That night, I stopped being so nervous as soon as I stepped out on the stage in my beautiful white gown. Out in the audience, I had my own personal cheering section. Just as my mother had come around once I was determined to be in the pageant, so had my entire family: both sets of my grandparents, my parents, my uncle John, and my aunt Judy. They also knew exactly what to do. At the top of their lungs they screamed, "YOU CAN DO IT, ABBEY!"

On the stage, the runways were not very wide. You had to walk up to where there was an *X* and turn, then walk to another *X* and turn again. Some girls had trouble walking with their super-high heels. Some looked scared of falling and had to remind themselves to smile.

I prayed and prayed so many times that I wouldn't fall. I came onstage, walking with the help of an escort.

The fair provided escorts for all the girls, and mine was really nice, but the fair had picked him, and I had never seen him before and haven't seen him since. When I got through the *X*s, I was so relieved and proud that I stood up tall, really tall, and all of a sudden the top of my dress slid down and I flashed the entire grandstand! I looked over at the panel judges and could see them mouthing, *"Oh my God . . . ,"* which always makes you feel wonderful and was actually very unprofessional of them, in my opinion. That's when I had to remind myself to smile.

My escort, who couldn't have been older than eighteen, grabbed the dress, and as he bent down to get it he whispered, "Do not cry." He held on to that dress and never let go of it the rest of the competition. He was a godsend. All the while, I could hear my grandpa Jack and grandma Wink cheering as loud as they could. I was so rattled and scared that they might be really embarrassed, but they kept cheering, and that helped. There were at least four hundred people in the grandstands and I had a bad feeling that every single one of them must have seen my dress fall, but then I told myself, *Well, what can you do?* Not long after that, Janet Jackson had the same problem, and hers was even worse because it happened when she was performing at the Super Bowl halftime show. Millions and millions of people saw her, so I figured I was in good company and that what had happened to me, by comparison, really wasn't so bad.

At that first pageant, I didn't take home a trophy, but I placed in the top ten out of thirty girls. The greatest part was that I got in the top ten and Rachel got in the top ten. I felt like I was equal to her for the first time. Our high school peers had put us at two different levels, Rachel's level being way higher than mine. So even though there were people in the world who thought I was a loser, there were other people who thought I was a winner.

That night, I realized a dream. I had achieved something that I—not to mention everyone else I knew—never thought was possible. From then on, I was all the more determined to do things I wanted to do, no matter what anyone else thought or said.

And, to tell you the truth, when the pageant judges put me in the top ten with Rachel, it was one of the really big events of my life because it made me realize that, in the end, the way you're perceived depends on who the judges are.

One strange thing I noticed at the pageant was that many girls—even the first runner-up—left the pageant in tears. Honestly, I think that's kind of crazy. Someone has to lose so someone can win. That's how a competition works.

Sure, in the moment, I was a little sad that I didn't get the crown, but by the time I got home I was already determined to enter more pageants, and I'd begun to imagine what I would do better next time: I'd work out harder, I'd make more eye contact, I'd be more confident, and I'd glue myself into my dress!

Plus, who had time to be sad? First thing in the morning, I was scheduled to go back to the fair because I had signed up my sheep Corbin and Kipper to be in the sheep show. If you ever want a unique experience, I suggest showing sheep.

FIVE

Journeys

I went to school with a girl named Carolyn who had severe CP. She walked with the aid of a walker, and her speech was somewhat slurred. She took a few classes in the main high school, but she was stuck in special ed the rest of the time. She always had an aide with her to help her. Her situation made me sad. Despite the fact that I wasn't cool, I could usually find some people—even the popular kids—who were nice enough to help me walk if I really needed it, or to carry my lunch tray, especially on soup day. I would have hated having an adult at my side every day, all day long. Carolyn didn't get to do things like pass notes to other girls in class or whisper funny things to her friends.

Because of Carolyn, I spent some time sitting in on the special ed classes. I wanted to see what it was like and how different it was from the kind of schooling all the other kids have. Well, from what I could see, special ed looked appalling! There was a bathroom in the classroom and a boy was sitting on the toilet with the door wide open. There was a girl lying on a bed. They were my age but they played with baby toys. I picked up a little keyboard, a toddler toy the colors of the rainbow, and handed it to a girl in a wheelchair to play with, but she wasn't allowed to have it. It was "too loud and distracting," so they gave her a freaking sock. Yes, a *sock* to play with. No wonder these kids seemed kinda "weird": They were trapped in a weird environment. I felt so bad for them. Just because they had CP or problems speaking or walking, people assumed they must be stupid. But I made a point of getting to know a lot of them, and from what I observed, their brains, in most cases, were just fine. But while we were learning Spanish, French, algebra, chemistry, and biology, they were singing kids' songs and learning to tell time. It just blew my mind.

Like so many of the challenged girls, Carolyn lived in that stifling world and, compared to the people I knew in high school, was so far behind. I always felt I had to talk to her as if I were talking to a three-year-old. I never felt free to joke with her or tease her in the way young girls tease each other. It wasn't her fault. It was like that mostly, I think, because her parents had decided she was not capable of doing anything that you or I would think of as normal, like having a friend or being on her own. Whenever I spent time with Carolyn, I would end up feeling bad for her and I would also feel thankful that my own parents had always treated me as if I didn't have a disability.

I hated the fact that Carolyn's life was so different from mine. She was so sweet and quiet and good. It broke my heart when she said she wanted to compete in the Miss Henry County pageant but that she couldn't because her parents thought people would make fun of her.

I wanted Carolyn to have the same opportunities I had. So, when I was in tenth grade and had just competed in the Miss Henry County pageant, I got the idea of staging a pageant for girls and young women whose special needs and disabilities make them feel inferior.

It turned out that creating a pageant from scratch is expensive. There were all sorts of things that had to be paid for: the rental fee for my high school's auditorium where the pageant would be held, a DJ to supply the music, decorations for the stage, souvenirs, T-shirts with the pageant's name on them to give as a thank-you gift to volunteers and participants, crowns, trophies, sashes, number buttons for each of the contestants, program books, and dinner for the contestants and the judges who had no time to go somewhere to eat in the short time between the afternoon rehearsal and the show at night. There were also posters to advertise and something I never would have thought of: insurance. I figured I needed about three thousand dollars to put on the pageant, and I didn't want to go to my family for the money. So I went to local businesses and asked if they'd be interested in donating. I thought I was going to be like Mary Kay and be a successful entrepreneur. As you know, I love Mary Kay. I had read her book at least a hundred times and I wore her makeup and even visited the Mary Kay headquarters in Dallas, Texas. Mary Kay was the first person who inspired me to chase after my dreams. The more I read about her, the more I believed in her motto, which was *One Woman Can!* While I was putting the pageant together, I would say that to myself over and over, and it really motivated me. I knew that she had inspired millions of women across the country to believe in themselves. Mary Kay had started with nothing and built a cosmetics empire all by herself. I wanted to do something like that with this pageant. But I was getting off to a pretty bad start, because the biggest check anyone gave me was for one hundred dollars, and after I had collected every penny I could, I was still two thousand dollars short.

So I went to my father, who really didn't get it, especially at first. That made me sad because it felt like my own dad really didn't have faith in me. I just wished that for once someone would take my visions seriously, but they didn't back then. Of course, I do give both my parents credit for letting me compete in the Miss Henry County pageant and cheering for me and buying me a really nice dress. And I had to admit that starting my own pageant was about one hundred times more complicated than that could ever be. I realized it was a giant project, bigger than anything I'd even thought about doing, and frankly, superbig when you consider I was only in tenth grade. But I was sure that once the pageant was over, my dad would feel what I felt about it. I hoped he would see the way the pageant was able to make a difference in the lives of the girls who were in it, even if it was just a little difference. I did understand his other concern, which was that organizing a pageant would take away from my schoolwork. I promised him it wouldn't, and I kept that promise. I also told him that I felt I was meant to do something that would help girls like Carolyn.

So I begged and pleaded with him. And even though he was pretty convinced I was in over my head and didn't have a whole lot of faith that the pageant would work out, I think he was also a little bit proud that I was taking it on, and he finally agreed to give me the extra two thousand dollars I needed to hold the first pageant.

It was small, just ten contestants. They were girls who had cerebral palsy or Down syndrome or severe autism. In terms of age, I figured the pageant should be for ages twenty-five and under; we had a twenty-three-year-old and a sixteen-year-old, and the rest were ten years old or younger than that. All but one contestant were local and that girl was from Peoria, which is only an hour away.

For this to be a real pageant, we needed judges, and because I was now competing in more pageants and had established some connections in that world, I was able to get a few local people to volunteer. One was a makeup artist, and another was the pageant coach I'd recently started working with. We also had Happy Joe Whitty, who is the owner of a chain of restaurants called Happy Joe's Pizza. The girls were to be judged and scored in four categories: Their private interview with the judges was 40 percent of their score, evening gown was 30 percent, the onstage question was 20 percent, and casual-wear was 10 percent.

Onstage, each girl was to be escorted by her father.

When they came out from the wings, each girl was absolutely beaming, and everyone in the audience was smiling—but with tears in their eyes. Even my dad was moved by what he saw, and by the time the winner was crowned I think he understood why this pageant meant so much to me. I will always be so grateful to him for making it possible.

I was really happy that Carolyn entered the contest. For the evening gown portion, she wore a strapless dress, and because her dad was helping her, she was able to get up out of her wheelchair and walk with a walker. Her short brown hair was pulled back with little barrettes in the shapes of butterflies. She looked so happy. She was first runner-up, and she was thrilled.

I knew it was a magical experience for all the girls, and I was really happy about that. The problem was that my school auditorium, where the event was held, seats eight hundred, and only forty seats were filled. When I first conceived the pageant, I was envisioning something so huge, something like Miss America with a stage full of roses and sparkly confetti falling down. This first time out, I couldn't come up with anything like that, but I was determined to have a bigger and better pageant the following year. I always try to be superoptimistic, and I was telling myself that everything I learned during the first pageant would help me with the next one. And there would definitely be a next one because, after seeing what the event had meant to the girls and their parents, there was no way on earth that I was going to stop at just one pageant.

The Miss You Can Do It pageant had become my dream. The timing was lucky, too—now that I was going into eleventh grade, I could finally take Mrs. Burke's entre-preneurship class. I had tried so many times to get into that class, but since it was only for juniors and seniors, I had had to wait. So finally, I was in the class, and I was really excited about finding out how to bring my dreams and visions to life. I was so happy once that class started because I just loved it so much. It was a class that made me believe anything was possible. It wasn't like math or English or any other academic course. It was unique and incredible and I was so eager to learn everything, so that eventually I would be able to expand my pageant and fulfill my dream of making it as big as Miss USA and Miss America.

When I was in entrepreneurship class, I sat in the very front row. If you knew me at all, you'd know that Abbey Curran does *not* sit in the front row. But this class was different. I'm not a halfway kind of person, and when I really like something I go all out, work my butt off, and give 110 percent attention.

That's what I did in entrepreneurship class, and it gave me the building blocks to create a dream come true. It taught me that every great idea begins with a business plan—not just for yourself, but so others can understand what you are trying to achieve, which can have the effect of making them more likely to help you and invest in you.

In addition to all the rest of my dreams, I have also always seen myself as a powerful businesswoman. I want to change the business world. I want to support those who don't have anybody to stand by them or just need someone who will give them the helping hand they deserve. I want to encourage people who dream of making something of themselves but are afraid they can't. I want to help the world to be less quick to judge and more ready to open their hearts a bit wider. I believe that business is one of the keys to achieving those things. I also believe that to be successful and reach out to as many people as possible, having a specific business plan is absolutely necessary.

In Mrs. Burke's class, we not only learned to make business plans, we also studied marketing and public relations, and I loved it all. Although I don't think I am especially good at every aspect of business, I do like to be creative, and this class made me feel like the sky's the limit! I had so many ideas and plans and I would work on this stuff for fun. Unfortunately, you need money or investors to get a new venture off the ground, and I had neither—but if I'd had them, I bet I would own about fifty self-made companies right now.

At my high school, at the end of each year all the students go to the auditorium, where the senior class is honored right before they graduate. This is when all the different awards are announced and handed out. They read the honor roll and give congrats to "such a great class president." After that are the sports awards: fastest runner, highest jumper, and on and on. The athletes all get big cut-out letter *K*s (for Kewanee), which they put on their varsity jackets. Well, I had watched this ceremony since freshman year, so I knew that Mrs. Burke gave a business award to the person most likely to be a successful entrepreneur. I knew I wasn't going to be getting any of the other awards, that's for sure, but that business award was one I thought I could win, and I set out to get it. After all, the Miss You Can Do It pageant was my own nonprofit, so that should count for something.

The truth is, I never considered the pageant to be a business. It was my calling, it was something I was driven to do, something I *had* to do for reasons that weren't at all about making money. But when I was fourteen, two years before I launched the pageant, I did have an entrepreneurial venture when I started Curran's Cosmetics. I had learned from Mrs. Burke that successful businesses find a "niche," and I thought maybe cosmetics could be mine. Mary Kay's motto *One Woman Can!* stuck with me. If she could start a cosmetics company, I thought why couldn't I do it, too?

Well, as it turned out, I couldn't.

One product I decided to make was perfume, so I ordered essences from an online distributor. One of the most popular scents is citrus, but I didn't want it because I don't think it's very attractive to smell like an orange. I wanted my perfume to be so sweet you'd wish it was edible, so I mixed "candy corn" essence with lilac. It was awful. It screamed old lady. But, hoping other people wouldn't think it was as bad as I did, I took it over to Twice as Nice, a resale shop for clothes and accessories that Mrs. Burke owned. She agreed to sell it, and over the next six months, she sold about twenty of them, including six my grandma bought for her friends. In case you ever make perfume, one tip I can give you is: Do not add glitter to it. I thought glitter was such a great original idea, but after a few days in the bottle, it formed into a hard clump like a little marble and kept the perfume from getting out.

The biggest nightmare was lip gloss. The main ingredient was petroleum jelly, which I had to boil and then mix with oils and fragrance. I worked in the kitchen and used my mother's good Calphalon pots, which were not ideal for this situation. Oil is hard to clean off surfaces and pure fragrances like lilac and lavender are super-strong and make your skin smell for a long time—and make your pots smell even longer. I swear, I spent more time cleaning the kitchen than making lip gloss. At first, I was so excited by the finished product and it actually sold pretty well, but no one was breaking the door down for more. Curran's Cosmetics hit rock bottom, and I realized that although I still thought I could be like Mary Kay, I would have to do it through a business that wasn't cosmetics.

When I began taking Mrs. Burke's entrepreneurship class in my junior year, I was already in the planning stage for the second pageant, and what she taught helped me then and still helps me to this day. I never looked for any personal "reward" for doing the pageant—my reward was the joy on the contestants' faces. But I know I did a really good job organizing and running the pageant, and those are business skills even when you're doing them for something you don't really see as a business. And the only thing I wanted in return was that business award. But I didn't get it. It went to a girl who had a 4.0 GPA in all of the business classes. She was nice and supersmart, and I'm sure she deserved it. But I was upset anyway.

That summer, I held the second Miss You Can Do It pageant and it went very well, thanks in part to what I had learned in my business classes. Mrs. Burke agreed to be a pageant judge, and she did such a great job of it and fit right in. I could tell that I had finally impressed her, which made me feel absolutely great. I thought it might lead to my getting the business award in my senior year, but that didn't happen either, even though Mrs. Burke liked the pageant so much she continued to be a judge at it for years after that. But in the end, getting the award was less important than the fact that my efforts to get it had spurred me on to work more and try harder. That was a big reward all by itself, because, as I've learned, what's most fulfilling isn't winning—it's doing your best.

Throughout my senior year, I was still learning a lot in entrepreneurship class and still loving every minute of it. Mrs. Burke taught us was what a nonprofit is, and how there are different categories—C Corp, S Corp, or LLC—and that if you ever start a nonprofit you have to file a 501(c)(3), which is what I had to do for my Miss You Can Do It pageant. That class also taught me how to market the pageant, how to advertise, and that I needed a mission statement, a vision statement, and a purpose— and yes, all three are different. As Mrs. Burke would say, "Look up the definition; you'll remember it then."

My own mission for the pageant was to provide an experience for challenged girls and young women that would give them a defining sense of accomplishment. My vision was to create a magical event that serves as a stepping stone for these young women and girls and helps them to realize that, if you believe in yourself, any dream can come true. And my overall purpose was to impart confidence to the girls by giving them an opportunity to prove they are able to do things they never thought possible.

Something else that helped me with my pageant was taking Typing 1 and 2. Typing class is something I feel to be a requirement, as thanks to typing I can write my pageant's marketing materials, create the script, and type contestants' resumes so quickly. Without typing class, it would take me so long that I would still be typing materials from the first pageant. I am so thankful for those courses. No one ever asks me about it, but I am a speed typist. I have the entire keyboard memorized and I can tell you what letter is in which spot on which line WITHOUT looking. I wish my high school had an award for speed typing!

Mrs. Burke understood how serious I was about the Miss You Can Do It pageant, which, when I was a high school senior, was about to have its third year. I asked her for advice on all sorts of things, such as what is the best way to raise money, and how to bargain with merchants in order to get a better price on things like crowns and sashes and T-shirts. She helped me a lot. Sometimes I think one reason I worked so hard on Miss You Can Do It was to impress her. Believe me, she is one hard woman to impress. Now, eight years after I graduated high school, I believe I have finally impressed her with everything I've done. But at the time, I don't think she was impressed with me, and I wanted her to look at me as someone who could use business skills in a creative way to enhance a pageant that had a really great chance of making a difference in a lot of lives.

I always felt the other students thought I was just a waste of Mrs. Burke's valuable time. But although they didn't see me as a person who could ever run a business, every day I spent in entrepreneurship class was making it more and more possible for me to do precisely that.

And that is one of the reasons I will be grateful to Mrs. Burke for the rest of my life.

The attitude of my classmates reminds me of a saying from a children's book that went something like: Just when the caterpillar thought the world was over, he turned into a butterfly. That's why I try not to underestimate anybody. You might dismiss them as a caterpillar, but they could become a butterfly the very moment you do.

One of the reasons I wanted to start the Miss You Can Do It pageant is my absolute belief that underestimating people is always a mistake. The disabled girls who entered the pageant often came to it feeling like caterpillars, but in fact they were butterflies, and every single one of them left knowing it.

The way I saw it, the pageant was not trying to make the girls into beauty queens but to encourage them to take part in new opportunities, to show them it's okay to take the risks and chances that are part of life's journey.

I was on a journey, too, entering other small beauty pageants that were held nearby, like Dream Girls USA. That was a fun one to be in because it has a queen for every category you compete in: swimsuit, evening gown, onstage question, runway model, and speech. I won in the speech category giving the same speech I'd been working on and was giving in other competitions. I talked about how every time someone tells me I can't do something, it's a lightning rod for action. I won a crown and a sash and was named Overall Spokesmodel Queen. It may not sound like much to you, but I was happy.

I was serious about the pageants. At first, I got pointers from a friend who had judged and helped in the pageant world for a long time. She knew about a real pageant coach who lived about thirty minutes from me, and I started going to the coach's home every week to practice things like how to sit, how to stand, how to put your feet in what they call a "T" so one foot is facing the audience and the other is facing the side.

She also taught me how to answer really silly questions like, "If you were ice cream, what flavor would you be and why?" And I had to answer quickly and not say "um"—you can never say "um." Instead, I would have to say something like, "I would be bubble gum, because bubble gum is so fun and exciting and pink is my favorite color."

And even though I know it's a totally ridiculous question and a more ridiculous answer, I would have to say it even if I hated ice cream and hated pink or was lactose intolerant because the judges are looking for girls who are smiley and perky and positive.

Of all the things the coach taught me, the one that

was hardest for me was that darn pageant walk. Gosh, how I want to walk like that! I have probably wanted to do it since the day I started walking. It's a confident, bouncy walk combined with a sexy swish of your butt and a saucy flip of your hair. I'll never understand why people who don't have CP don't walk like that all the time. It screams beauty and confidence, and I sure wish the way I walk screamed both of those things. I used to practice this fantastic walk in my kitchen in my socks. It is definitely easier to do in socks on a slippery floor than on a runway in heels, but no matter how many times I try it, I haven't even come close to getting it 100 percent right. I sometimes think that maybe the reason I was given cerebral palsy is that if I didn't have it, I might have become a cocky, hair-flipping, fancy-walking girl, and then I might have overlooked so many incredible people and things. I wouldn't understand how you can ache for hours when you're pitied for having a condition you didn't choose. I wouldn't understand how shallow so many people can be. I wouldn't have known that the girl in school who is judged because she lives in public housing should be judged on the contents of her heart.

The year after I was in the Miss Henry County competition, my coach was preparing me for the Hog Days festival. At the festival, you had to give a one-minute speech, and if you wanted to win, your speech had to be related to agriculture. So my speech was about growing up on a hog farm and being a hog farmer's daughter and then making my usual statement of my own philosophy by saying, "Whenever people tell me I can't do something, it's a lightning rod for action."

The first year I entered, I got first runner-up, which I thought was the coolest thing ever. The second year, I won. I truly and totally won! It was the first thing I had ever won in my entire life (except for those pony contests that I didn't exactly win, since Grandpa Jack had paid off the judges). The title was Miss World Festival, which was a lot better than being called Miss Hog Days or something like that. Actually, the title used to be Miss Pork Chop, but I guess the people who run the pageant figured out that it wasn't the kind of title any girl would want. I got a crown and a white sash with *Miss World Festival* written on it in black writing. And I got to be queen of Hog Days and ride in an open car during the Hog Days Parade, which was pretty darn exciting.

Winning was so awesome that I wanted to win more! I started doing whatever I could to prepare for pageants and help my chances once I got there. I worked out a lot and got my complexion cleared up and took good care of myself by getting enough sleep and eating a lot of protein and vegetables and salads. Because I was trying to be a pageant girl I also did some things that I know really aren't good for you, like going to tanning booths and drinking SlimFast. Those are not things I would ever recommend to anyone, and as soon as I stopped competing in pageants, I never did them again.

Something else that helped me was that I kept going to see the coach, who would tell me to smile more, to do more hand gestures when I was giving a speech, to talk slower, to sit upright and put my hands in my lap, and always remember to make eye contact.

One time I had a blue swimsuit I wanted to wear at a local contest, but she wanted me to buy a brown one that she said would look better on me. Blue is my favorite color and brown is the color of pig poop, so I was definitely picking blue. There was no way I was going to wear a brown swimsuit, even if it said I should on my color wheel—which she was always referring to. Then there was my hair: In local pageants you're always supposed to wear your hair up. But why would I do that? It made me look like a cue ball.

Still, I did listen to every word the coach said, and with the exceptions of my hair and the blue swimsuit, I followed her instructions. I think that's a pretty big deal, because I have done some pageant coaching over the past few years and my girls never listen to a word I say. Coaching isn't easy. One thing I learned from doing it is to have so much respect for people who've taken on the task of coaching me. As much as I wanted to win, I told myself that the most important thing was to go out onto the pageant stage and do your best and take a chance. And—nearly all the time—I believed this.

That simple but important idea—to do your best and take a chance—was one of many things I was determined to instill in my Miss You Can Do It girls. As I graduated high school and prepared to go to college, I knew that I wanted to continue Miss You Can Do It and to keep pushing myself to enter more pageants and get farther in them than I had before.

SIX

College

I went to Saint Ambrose University in Davenport, Iowa. In my heart I knew that someday I would want to follow in the footsteps of my mother and both of my grandmothers and become a nurse, because that is such a direct way to be of help to people. But I had also realized by then that I could be of help by becoming a reporter who covered stories about those who are challenged and people who are suffering in any number of ways. So in college I decided to major in communications. Most of my homework was speechwriting, marketing plans, and public speaking.

I had really wanted to go to college. I wasn't at all scared about being away from home and being on my own. Luckily, my family always believed I'd be just fine. They knew that I always take really good care of myself.

When I'm hungry, I eat; when I'm tired, I sleep; when I need to go someplace, I drive there. Also, I don't drink or smoke, and, unfortunately, hadn't yet had a date. So when I say there was less than nothing to worry about, I really mean it.

The funny thing was that, while they weren't worried about me, I was very concerned about my family, because by that time, I had taken on all sorts of tasks to help out. I kept thinking, *When I'm not there, who will take Grandma into town to get her hair done? Who will spend the afternoon with Grandpa Jack? What if Dad needs a tractor moved or the yard mowed? What if my mother needs to have the laundry washed and pressed?* These were some of the activities I had gotten in the habit of doing all the time. Some people were surprised that I could do anything physical on my dad's farm, but to me, that's just another example of a "disabled" person being underestimated.

In college, I wasn't the only person with a disability. There were three others, though one of them was way too cool for me, and so pretty it was easy to look past the fact that she was disabled. But while I never saw any signs of disability, she said she had CP, so it must have been very mild. The disabilities of the two other girls were totally apparent: One walked with two canes, and the other had an electric wheelchair. I was friendly with them, but not good friends, though everyone figured we'd all be the best of friends just because each of us lived with a physical challenge. Frankly, that really annoyed me. It was another assumption made by people who looked at me and saw only my disability and defined me by it. I was determined to fight those misconceptions and to prove that, if someone defines a disabled person in that way, all they've revealed is their own ignorance.

Being in a college and having CP was okay at certain times and not so okay at others. I had to put up with the people who stared at me, and the ones who ignored me, and the ones I disliked the most because they made fun of me. But I also met one of my best friends ever in college, and she became one of my roommates. She was one of the people who didn't make a big deal about my CP, and I was really grateful for that. Still, I almost always felt left out. I wanted to be fun and popular, and it just wasn't happening. Most of all, I was a little sad that I didn't get any college experiences with guys. My roommates would bring cute guys back to our room, and the guys would be flirting with them and would barely even look at me. I figured out pretty quickly that my chances of getting an actual date were slim to none. It seemed like most people thought I wasn't supposed to be someone who could have a good time. I was supposed to be a saint because I'm disabled. Even today most people think I'm supposed to be serious about everything and sit home and read the Bible. I mean, there are times when I really do like to be at home with my pets and have a quiet night. But there are other times when I'd like to let loose and have a great time. I wish people would understand that a disabled person is really and truly a person—just like them.

Every day of college, I got a parking ticket. The reason for this was that even though the school parking lots were pretty big, there was only one handicapped parking spot in each one and 99.9 percent of the time, I didn't get it. This might seem like a small thing to you, but it was a big problem for me! Not getting that parking spot ruined my day. It meant I had to walk across the parking lot and then the campus dragging my huge book bag while people stared at me. Some even mimicked the way I walk. If one of them had let me lean on their arm, it would have meant the world to me. But they didn't. They'd run by me, then turn around and stare. When I have kids, I will do my best to teach them it's all right to be different. I love children and I feel like I will be a good mom. I'll tell my kids, "Don't be afraid of falling or failing; I'll be there to stitch up the scrapes and cuts. Be nice to everyone you meet and remember that friends come in all shapes, sizes, colors, and ages and may have some sort of challenge."

But these kids stared at me like they were thinking, *What's her problem? She's weird.*

Trust me: I hate my walk more than anyone else possibly could hate it. But it doesn't make me weird. The way I see it is, everyone is different. Even though you might find something "weird" about someone, I am sure someone can find something "weird" about you. So why not just drop the whole idea of weirdness and accept people as they are?

I had really hoped that things would be different at college than they'd been in high school, and I was really disappointed to discover that I was as much of an outcast as I'd been before. It was as if people thought CP must be contagious. Every day, after trudging across campus and trying to ignore the mimicry and the mean stares, I'd get to class late and sweaty and feeling that no one cared and no one understood. By the time anyone saw me in class, I looked pathetic. I'd rip off my coat and the entire back of my shirt would be wet and I'd look like something was really wrong with me. It was so embarrassing. But I couldn't help it. Walking was a real workout for me and still is.

It seemed to me that most people on that campus were as cold as the temperature on a January day. So after a while, I started to skip some classes; as far as I was concerned, I had to do way too much walking for one fifty-minute class. If I stayed in my dorm, I could shut the door, and no one stared. My roommate Sarah was a really great person. She accepted me fully, to the point that if I asked her to do something to help me she'd say, "No. Do it yourself." That was good for me. But if I really, truly needed help, she'd do it.

Every morning at school I'd wake up early to take a shower, curl my hair, and do my makeup. I'm not sure why I did all this—I guess it was either because or in spite of the fact that I had never been on a date and never been kissed. I was the only person I knew who had never been kissed, and it was bothering me more and more. There were a few times when a guy was interested in me, but only because he met me when I was sitting down. As soon as I would have to get up and walk, I knew he'd be thinking something was seriously wrong with me. On the plus side, one of my main goals is to learn from any bad experience. Here's what I learned in that case: You can't wait for Prince Charming to change your life. That fairy tale was written for children long ago; in my life, I can write my own fairy tales, and although it would be incredible to have a man in my life who really loved me, the bottom line is I don't need a prince to make my dreams come true.

Another thing I learned in my college years is that crying doesn't fix anything. Even when I felt moments of the worst kind of sadness, I would tell myself that I needed to stay positive, *especially* when it's a struggle. I had to keep on keeping on because that's the only way to turn sadness into determination.

Back when I was twenty and basically miserable because I had never had a boyfriend, I met a man who was a lot older than I was who wanted to "date" me. Of course, I would have loved to have had a boyfriend in high school, or during my first years of college, but that wasn't going to happen since as far as boys were concerned, I basically didn't exist. So it took meeting someone older—and maybe wiser and more tolerant—to finally get my first date. I thought I was on top of the world. Finally, a man had asked me out, had wanted to be with me, even though he knew I had CP and had seen me limp. He was a doctor, and it was a really big deal for someone like me who had never been able to get a date, even with some would-be cowboy who hung out at the Sale Barn.

But after we'd had a couple of dates, I realized he was

seeing another person, too. For a girl who had never had a boyfriend that was truly heartrending. I sat in my dorm crying. Was I ever going to be anybody's number one?

But then, after a few days of crying (stupid move, but young and stupid I was), I got angry and used that anger to get myself fired up. I went to the gym every day. I worked out so hard. The rage I felt pushed me through every weight I lifted, through every moment on the elliptical. Working out was the greatest therapy ever, and after a while I wasn't angry anymore. Actually, I realized how lucky I am that he didn't pick me, because I don't want a man who dates another woman when he's dating me. I want a man who wants me and only me, because I am good enough inside and out. Maybe I'll find that and maybe I won't, but either way, I will be okay.

The best times I had in college were when I hung out with Sarah and our friends Cassie and Tom. We had so much fun decorating our rooms with flashing pink and blue Christmas lights—they were so beautiful that we never took them down. We also would throw great parties for ourselves on Saint Patrick's Day, when we'd get all dressed up in green clothes and eat lots of cupcakes with green icing. On Halloween, we would all go to so-called haunted houses where there were fake ghosts and skeletons and cobwebs and all sorts of fun, scary things.

But my parents hadn't sent me to college to get a boy-friend or to just have fun. And the odd thing was that the more fun I had, the more I got confused and wor-ried. Where was my life going? What was I going to be? I didn't want to feel like nobody special.

SEVEN
Creating a Pageant

If you had asked me when I was in college what I wanted most, I would have told you the same thing I would say if you asked me that today: I want to make a difference in the world. I wanted to do something fantastic! I wanted to help people. And the one way I found to do it was the Miss You Can Do It pageant, which, by the time I was a freshman in college, was entering its fourth year. By then, I had my basic operating system all worked out, and as soon as Christmas had come and gone, I would start to plan the pageant for the coming summer. The first thing I always do is contact Easter Seals. They're a great organization that provides help to kids who are disabled. Most of the girls for my pageant come to it through Easter Seals, and the others come because they've heard about the pageant or they have a friend who had been in it.

Every year, I went to the owners of local businesses and asked them to donate whatever money they could. I then lined up people to be the judges. My ideal judges were women or men who really understood pageants. So I was lucky to get people like Judi Ford Nash, who had been Miss America in 1969 and lives one town away from my home in Kewanee. I also had a local TV reporter and—as I mentioned—my teacher Mrs. Burke, as well as some excellent local dermatologists and makeup artists. The pageant was usually held in August, during summer break. I would order decorations, and the week before the girls arrived, I would deck out my high school auditorium with lots of help from my mother and grandma and people I'd invited to be on the pageant's board of directors.

From the beginning, I had decided that the theme of Miss You Can Do It should always be Utopia, so we decorate my old high school auditorium in silver and blue with lots of big cutout stars. There are giant silver arches covered in shiny blue stars, another arch made up entirely of sparkling stars in white and silver and blue, and the trophies are displayed on five-foot columns. Everything sparkles; everything is shiny and bright. The idea is to make something more than just a pageant; we create a magical realm where the girls can feel special and wish on stars and dream big and know they've entered a world where everyone has a chance and an equal opportunity to win.

The pageant has grown each year, getting bigger as more and more people hear about it and tell their friends, who tell their friends. The best part of it is that it's reaching girls with every sort of personality and every sort of challenge. There was the five-year-old with spinal muscular atrophy who could not stand or walk unaided, but it didn't keep her from enjoying her toys and her coloring books and her siblings; there was the seven-year-old quadriplegic who was excited by the fact that she was learning how to add and subtract and read; and there was the sweet, shy eight-year-old born with Down syndrome who held my hand so tight.

It is the most moving thing in the world to see these girls looking so proud and thrilled and pretty as they come onto the stage wearing frothy pink or white or yellow dresses, their hair held with pastel-colored ribbons. Some are in wheelchairs, some have braces on their legs, some are pushing walkers, some are supported by canes. What they have in common is the look of radiant happiness as the audience applauds them. These are girls who rarely, if ever, get the kind of positive feedback other children get. Yet here they are, the center of so much loving attention, bubbling over with so much joy that you'd think they might burst!

I have it set up so that everyone wins an award for participating, and then there are a bunch of other awards: best private interview, casualwear, evening gown, best answer to the onstage question, and most photogenic, as well as Miss Congeniality, fourth runner-up, third runner-up, second runner-up, first runner-up, and Queen. And every girl in the pageant gets a sash and a crown, so I don't think anyone has ever gone away disappointed.

All the girls hold their trophies up high and they smile so big, even when they win something small like most photogenic, that you'd think they had won Queen. For me, the very best part of Miss You Can Do It is watching the Queen get crowned. She is given the crown by the winner from the year before, and it's so touching that everyone in the auditorium starts weeping and even the Little Miss You Can Do It Queen cries, which really gets to me. It's one of my favorite moments, because it's when she and all the other girls feel they're on top of the world. At the very end of the pageant, I play Tina Turner's "Simply the Best" as loud as possible because these girls *are* the best! And confetti falls and it's magical!

I was always looking for celebrity judges, and when I

was planning the fourth competition in 2007, I managed to get the phone number of Shirley Cothran Barret, who had been Miss America in 1975.

What can I say? I look up to beauty queens. I admire them because they're not only beautiful but also disciplined, and they carry themselves with the kind of self-assurance I've always wanted to feel. I was constantly searching the Miss USA and Miss America websites to find out what these beautiful girls were doing with their lives because whatever it was, it would give me ideas for things I might want to accomplish and make me ever more determined to do them. The websites showed all of their pictures and told me about what they were doing at the time. And, to me, Shirley was the most impressive because she was not only a wife and the mother of four children, and had earned a doctorate degree in early childhood education and counseling, but she had also become a keynote speaker with a great message that I first learned about on her website. She said, "The motivation in our lives is the 'grit' within us, enabling us to tackle the impossible when everyone else is telling us to give up. In a world that always has 'an exception to the rule' it is imperative to never give up and take the easy way, but to continually point ourselves in the direction of productivity, growth, and achievement."

It was a message that mirrored all the things I had come to believe, and I'm not exaggerating when I tell you that it sent chills to my heart.

I felt that I needed something really special for my Miss You Can Do It girls. And I couldn't think of anyone more special than Shirley Barret. I wanted this Miss America to be one of the judges! I went to her website, found a phone number, and called it immediately. The person I spoke with was a very cordial man by the name of Richard who turned out to be her husband. I asked Richard if Shirley could come and judge the Miss You Can Do It pageant, and I gave him all of the details: You arrive on Friday and leave on Sunday; you fly into Chicago or the Quad Cities and we drive you to Kewanee; you stay—believe it or not—at the local furniture store, where there are four really beautiful sample bedrooms that are rented out like hotel rooms. These rooms have double canopy beds and Jacuzzis and beautiful lamps and mirrors and rugs and the only funny thing about them is that everything in them is for sale.

Richard said he would look into it. Days passed and nothing. So I called him again. He said he didn't know yet, and so a few more days passed and I tried again. He finally said the words that I could not believe— "Here's Shirley!" Holy smokes! I was sitting in my dorm room with Sarah and Cassie at the time and I remember screaming with excitement and how we were all laughing like crazy and jumping up and down. *The* Shirley Barret was about to be on the phone with me! I was so nervous I thought I'd keel over, but she sounded like such a nice lady and we actually talked for some time about all the amazing things she does. She told me that the weekend the pageant was scheduled for didn't work for her.

I said, "Okay, when does? I need you at the pageant."

She was really amazing: She gave me the date of another weekend and I told her we'd have the pageant then and all of a sudden—as easily as that—it was settled. When I hung up, Cassie, Sarah, and I started jumping around the room and screaming again. They were so excited for me. That summer, I felt like a kid waiting for Christmas, and the closer it got to the pageant, the more excited I was about meeting Miss America. To tell you the truth, I was so looking forward to seeing her that I couldn't even sleep. I will never forget waiting for her outside the furniture store and seeing the car that brought her from the airport slow to a stop. Then the door opened and out came this beautiful, elegant, smiling lady. All I could do was hug her! She was wonderful and kind and very Southern, calling me Sweet Abbey and asking for biscuits and gravy when we went out to eat.

She would become the person who singlehandedly changed my life.

At the Miss You Can Do It pageant, she gave a speech. She said, "Accomplishment begins with two words: 'I'll try.' All of us build walls in our own heads, and those walls can keep us from being everything we can possibly be and set us up for failure. Sometimes we just need to step up to the plate and swing that bat. We might strike out, we might get a home run, or we might only get to first base, but the point is we will never know unless we try. And remember: A true Queen doesn't give up!"

The faces of those girls lit up as Shirley spoke. It was clear that she really got to them. Her words were also exactly what I needed to hear. From that day on, whenever I had to deal with doubters who were so sure I couldn't do anything, I would remember what Shirley said, and then I'd repeat to myself the words that had become my mantra: *You don't think I can . . . well, watch me!* Someday I think I'll have those words put on T-shirts and give them to anyone I meet who has any kind of challenge, to inspire them just as Shirley inspired me. I can never thank Shirley enough for what she gave to me and my girls.

I had great hopes for the pageant. I could see how much being there meant to the girls and their parents.

I felt so grateful for this opportunity to encourage these sweet girls and give them something to be happy about. The pageant filled a need for them, and it did the same for me: It had become my way of making a difference in this world.

EIGHT
Dreams

A lot of the time I feel that I'm supposed to be chipper and perky and say that the world is perfect and that everyone always believed in me and in my dreams. I wish that were true. If I were to write that, this book would be fiction. Still, I always had dreams, and nobody could take them away from me, no matter how foolish anyone thought they were. No one ever thought I could be Miss Iowa or start a pageant of my own, but I accomplished those things because my dreams were huge, and they still are. One reason I loved business classes so much was because every great business—be it Disney or Mary Kay—was begun by one person with a big dream.

When I had visited the Mary Kay headquarters in Dallas, Texas, I thought it was the most breathtaking building I had ever seen. It's like Disney World for grown-ups, with beautiful water fountains and a huge pink Cadillac SUV parked out front. The building was all trimmed in gold, with splashes of ice pink everywhere. The carpet, if you look closely, is actually ice-pink roses spun in with gray.

When you walk in, there is a huge black wall with Mary Kay's motto, *One Woman Can!*, written on it in gold. The whole place is so gorgeous that it is the inspiration for my own dream of creating a hospital center for women. I'm proud of what Miss You Can Do It has been able to accomplish, but I don't want to stop there. My other really big idea is to create an ideal hospital, where patients can feel like human beings, and outpatients can come to have every sort of problem or ailment treated in a beautiful environment by loving, caring people.

I have it all worked out: The hospital building would be nestled in the outskirts of Chicago where there are lots of beautiful tall trees.

You'd drive up to it through a special path that would be festooned with white twinkling lights, and then you'd pull up in the big circular driveway, which would be lined with inspirational flags that read "Believe" and "Dream" and "Hope" and "Wish."

In the center of the main lobby, there would be a

woman playing a beautiful white piano surrounded by delicate white cages with yellow canaries in them. There would be carts lined up so that visitors could sit in them as they took a ride through the Miss You Can Do It pageant museum. These carts would be like golf carts, only the seats would be gold leather and the carts themselves would be pink.

You would have many choices at this center. If you decided to take the glass elevators to a lower floor, where all the doctors were, you'd pass huge tanks filled with tropical fish the whole way down. You could see whatever kind of doctor you needed to see—an internist, a dermatologist, an eye doctor. Whatever you choose, your wait time would be no more than fifteen minutes and the cost would be way lower than you'd find anywhere else.

There would also be a cafeteria with free jumbo cookies, and cupcakes with all different kinds of icing. Upstairs, there would be the Miss You Can Do It pageant museum, designed to inspire anyone with a disability, and also to show the so-called normal people that disabled girls can do things you wouldn't think they could do. The pure white walls would be covered with photographs of every one of the Miss You Can Do It contestants and Queens, and you would be able to tell from their glowing smiles that they are proud to be who they are. The floors would have silver sparkles in them so when sunlight comes through the dome ceiling, they would twinkle and shine. There would also be a theater where you could watch inspirational movies and hear motivational speakers. Next door to it would be a large office where staff members can sit down with you and order you your favorite clothes from our amazing clothing line. We would have everything from skinny jeans to gowns to crop tops to spandex workout attire, all with special magnets instead of zippers so even people with severe disabilities can slide into the coolest clothes and no one will know the difference.

Then you might want to go to the room where you get fitted for your custom wheelchairs, walkers, braces, bikes, book bags, and more. Keep in mind that the walkers won't look like walkers and wheelchairs won't look like wheelchairs. They will be nice to look at, and you won't have to feel embarrassed when you use them. These wouldn't be just for people with special needs; it might be that a high school football player just got hurt and wants something cool to wheel around in while he recovers. We would have fifteen colors to choose from, with the options of lights, sparkles, iPod docks, Wi-Fi connections, all for your wheelchair, braces, or walker. The room where you make these choices would be ivory and pastel pink with a giant fireplace and a mantelpiece with angels carved into it. We would also have a room where you could come and talk to me and my pageant board about anything. Maybe you are feeling depressed about your disability, and you and your parents wonder if the pageant would be good for you; maybe you are getting made fun of in school and you want to come in and tell us about it and get us to come to your school and teach the kids about bullying. So you sit there in this beautiful room and relax, and everything feels better to you than it did before. I know as well as anyone does how difficult it is to live with a disability. That is why one of my dreams is to offer the soothing, kindly, helpful environment I've always wanted for myself. Some people think my dreams are amazing and other people think I'm crazy. But I only listen to those people who are brave enough to go after dreams of their own.

Even if other people don't think much of my dreams, nobody can stop me from dreaming. I've dreamed that my opinion matters. I've dreamed that someone wants to listen to what I have to say. All of these dreams have come true to one extent or another. To me, my only unrealistic dream is to walk like everyone else.

Anytime someone goes out of their way to do something nice for me, I appreciate it so much. Those people are just sensational, and I dream that everyone could be like them. Why can't we always imagine what it would be like to be in someone else's situation? Why can't we open doors for each other and exchange smiles? I understand that many people aren't motivated to do these things because a lot of the time nobody notices, or the action isn't reciprocated. But these are the things I dream of.

There was one other dream I'd had since I was a little kid: Every year, I watched the Miss USA and Miss America pageants and dreamed of being that girl on TV who won the crown.

NINE
Taking a Chance

In the fall of 2007, when I was in my sophomore year, I got a flyer for the Miss Iowa USA 2008 pageant. I hung it up in my dorm room because it was so pretty. So tempting. But even though I had competed in quite a few pageants by then, the only title I had ever won was Miss World Festival, formerly known as Miss Pork Chop. And that was just a little local pageant—this one was major. There was also a very big entry fee, and the only way I could come up with it would be to get it from my parents, who I knew would be shocked at the price. The pageants I had entered before either didn't require an entry fee or cost one hundred dollars. Miss Iowa cost almost seven hundred dollars. That was a lot, but it's expensive to enter these larger pageants because they cost a fortune to run, and the entry fees are used toward those expenses. This was a really huge pageant and, in my mind, the most important one, especially since whoever wins gets to compete in the Miss USA pageant, and the winner of that gets to compete for Miss Universe.

Each year, about fifty girls get chosen for the pageant. In my year there were fifty-four. Anyone can apply who fits the basic criteria: You have to be single, never been married, and never had a child; you can't be older than twenty-six; you can't have a criminal record; and you have to be a US citizen. Also, you don't have to represent the state you were born or raised in, but you have to have lived there for a year. Because I had spent a year at college in Iowa, I qualified for the Miss Iowa competition.

I wanted to enter but couldn't decide if it would be worth it to spend all that money. When I asked my former pageant coach, she said, "Some people are meant for the NFL and some aren't, and I don't think you are meant for this."

I'd like to say her words came as a shock, but they didn't. As I've said, it's always been hard for other people to believe I could do anything—which, by the time I was thinking of entering the Miss Iowa competition, had become extremely depressing. But it also was one of those lightning rods for action that I had spoken about on pageant stages, so instead of wallowing in it, I geared up once again to prove them all wrong. Plus, when you don't hear what you want to hear, the only sensible thing to do is to get a second opinion.

My second opinion came from Shirley Cothran Barret, who remains one of the most amazing people I have ever had the pleasure of meeting.

A month after Shirley came to Kewanee to judge the pageant I called her and told her I was thinking about entering the Miss Iowa competition. I said I was nervous. I asked her, "What will happen if I fall?"

She said, "So what if you fall? You should do it. Don't let this opportunity slip by."

To have a former Miss America encouraging me made everything seem so different. Okay . . . I wasn't cool; I wasn't popular; I wasn't getting straight As—but a former Miss America was on the phone with me and she was my supporter and my friend.

After that, the parking problem at college no longer mattered to me. I made it to class every day with a smile on my face; a lot of the time I was smiling so much just because I had managed to get to class instead of hiding in my dorm room. And I took a chance and entered the Miss Iowa USA pageant. I didn't know I was the first girl with a physical challenge to be in the pageant. With so many people telling me I shouldn't do it, of course I was scared to enter. I just had to get over it. The truth is, I'm still not over thoughts like those, but if I'm ever going to get anywhere in this world, I have to fool myself into believing I am.

The main thing was that I refused to be one of those people who look back and say "what if."

That year, Miss America was a gorgeous blonde named Lauren Nelson. I decided she would be my template, even though she had been a Dallas Cowboys cheerleader and I couldn't qualify for the Kewanee High School cheerleading squad. That's how far apart we were. But it's what made me work so hard.

I got a personal trainer. I was nervous about it because training meant walking, running, using my legs, and balancing—the hardest things for me to do. I knew I would have to lean on him and use him for balance a lot right off the bat, but Keith was such a great guy that I trusted him almost from the start. He was just a little bit older than I was, and he was different from so many other people I'd known: He didn't underestimate me, he believed I could realize my dreams, and he never made me feel stupid about having them.

When I had difficulties in the gym and thought what he wanted me to do was way too hard, he'd say, "Yes, it's hard for everybody. Now do it." He was tough, and that was really good for me because it proved that he wasn't pitying me like the kids had back in grammar school when they were afraid to throw the dodgeball at "the crippled girl." When he was tough on me, it reminded me a lot of my dad, who had helped me so much by not making allowances for my CP—which is one of the reasons I've never used CP as an excuse for anything, with the exception of walking.

Keith was so encouraging. He really wanted me to do well, and I felt so good making him proud. He would always stand behind me and promise he wouldn't let me fall, and he always kept his word. And he didn't laugh when I brought him pictures of Lauren and asked him, "How do I get these abs? How do I get these arms?" Instead, he showed me the exercises that bring about the best results. I didn't think I could ever be as beautiful as Lauren Nelson, but I also knew it was important to do everything in my power to try.

Another thing that was lucky for me was that the people at Soderstrom Skin Institute wanted to get involved in my preparation. Dr. Soderstrom is a dermatologist and his associate Dr. Lomax is a plastic surgeon. The institute has five separate locations in the Midwest, one of which is near Kewanee. They offer every kind of skin service you could ever want or imagine. When I was getting ready for Miss Iowa, they basically said, "Give Abbey whatever she wants."

The institute's slogan is "Simply Beautiful," and the technicians and doctors there helped me a lot: They removed my chicken pox and acne scars, and cleared my skin with this miracle injection called Kenalog. They also gave me glycolic peels and high-frequency facials and tips about what brands of makeup to use. It was pretty amazing. I'd never even had a facial before, and I sure as heck had never been pampered before. They helped transform me into a pageant girl who could genuinely compete for the title of Miss Iowa.

From the time I sent in my entry form until the pageant, I had three months to prepare. It motivated me to look at pictures of Lauren, who was gorgeous. When I got tired at the gym I'd tell myself, *Lauren wouldn't stop working out just because she was exhausted.*

Every day, I woke up at 5:00 a.m. to hit the gym before I went to class. I had never worked so hard. I would spend two hours every day on the stair stepper. I always used the stair stepper instead of the treadmill because on the treadmill I would have to walk, and for me, walking is harder than any workout, even a really intense one.

One thing that helped me a lot is that Keith treated me as if I had already won Miss Iowa and was preparing for Miss USA. When I'd tell him, "I can't do this machine for one more second!" he'd sneak behind me and say, "Well, too bad, because I'm pretty sure Miss Iowa can."

That would give me the energy to get back on the machine and work even harder.

Another person who is truly gorgeous is a blue-eyed brunette named Deidre Downs, who was Miss America 2005. She was so stunning, and one of her gowns was the most amazing one I ever saw. I did an internet search for "where did Deidre Downs get her gown," and the name Sherri Hill popped up. It turned out that Sherri Hill designs and makes gowns for hundreds of beauty contestants and sells perfect copies of the gowns after they appear in them.

I begged my dad to buy me a copy of Deidre's dress. I love my dad, but every time I would say something big or grand he'd say, "Hold on. Let me buckle up before we head out to dream world." That was a joke, but it hurt my feelings. But then that was how a lot of people reacted when I talked about my dreams. It just made me want to try harder. I told my dad that being in the Miss Iowa pageant was an experience that would never come again, and after a lot of begging he gave in. I was so happy about this—except for the fact that whenever he does something major for me, he makes me do something in exchange, and it's usually something I would rather not do. So this time it was mow the yard a few times a week and sit in the front row at church with Grandma, even though being trapped in the front row at church gives me cold sweats. I suppose it was a fair trade when you consider how much the dress cost, and how nice it was of my dad to buy it for me.

But it was worth it. The gown was stunning. Deidre's dress had been purple; mine was peacock blue but exactly like hers, with thousands of gorgeous crystals and lots of chiffon. When it arrived in the mail, it was better than I could have dreamed. I told my dad that if I was going to ever win a pageant, it was going to be in this gown. To this day, it is still the most beautiful thing I have ever set eyes on.

I can see how you might think that preparing for a beauty pageant is only about the way you look. But it's actually about much more, because how you look physically can really be a reflection of how disciplined and how goal-oriented you are, and those are two qualities that you can—and should—apply to every single aspect of your life. For instance, even as I was gearing up for the Miss Iowa pageant, I was still studying for my bachelor's degree in business communications. And the discipline I needed in the gym really helped me at school, where I was now getting A's and B's and where I was more determined and focused than I had ever been.

So even though I was busting myself to "look good," a pageant, for me, will always be about a whole lot more than the parts of a person that you can see.

The three months of preparation passed quickly. Working with Keith got better every day, despite the times when it all seemed way too hard for me. The great thing was that hard times give you an opportunity to push through them. Every time I had wanted to give up—but didn't—I counted as a success. As far as the pageant was concerned, I honestly never believed that winning was an option. I thought that maybe I could place in the top five, which would be so incredible—and I would have been pretty happy with the top ten, too. I told myself that no matter what happened, just being there was a win, because it was such an unbelievable experience.

Getting ready for the Miss Iowa pageant was a very special time in my life, and I wanted to be sure I would remember each and every moment. So on the evening before I left for the pageant, I brought my camera to the gym and took pictures of Keith, and of every piece of equipment I'd worked out on, and of the local Subway where every night during those three months of training I had eaten the same dinner of chicken breast with peppers, lettuce, and tomato on wheat bread and sometimes a pickle, even though it was supersalty.

With the competition just one day away, I was getting more scared by the minute about what it would be like: How would they treat me? Would the other girls be nice to me? Could I handle the intimidation and all the pressure?

TEN
The Miss Iowa Pageant

On Thanksgiving night 2007, my mom and dad, my childhood friend Tessa, and I hit the road, driving three hours through a fierce snowstorm to Ottumwa, Iowa, where the pageant would be held.

Finally, we got to the official pageant hotel and checked in. It was late, and all I wanted to do was try to stay calm and get a good night's sleep.

The next day was the "prelims," which is the set of events that allow the pageant judges to decide which girls will be in the top ten. All fifty-four of the contestants would take part in prelims and compete in front of an audience in each of the established categories: swimsuit, evening gown, and onstage question. There was also a private interview with the judges that would take place before the live show. By the end of prelims, all but ten of those girls will have been cut by the judges. The top ten girls who are left would be announced the following night at the actual pageant, where the winner will be crowned.

In the car, on the way to the venue with my dad, I sent texts to Keith and to Shirley Barret. They read, "Here we go! Wish me luck!" They both answered right away. Keith wrote, "Good luck, Miss Iowa 2008!" Shirley's text read: "You can do this!" Those replies were so meaningful to me. Sometimes, when I don't have faith in myself, the one thing that gets me through is being reminded that other people have faith in me.

When we finally reached the Bridge View Center, where the pageant would be, my dad walked me to the door just as he always had when I went to school. I was absolutely terrified. Each time the door of the center opened, I could see the tall, thin girls inside, rocking sweatpants and walking around in hot rollers and very high heels. Other girls walked by me carting tons of baggage: big mirrors, hair dryers, giant comforters for napping. I had brought little more than the pageant basics: my dress, which was on a hanger; a little carry-on-size bag containing makeup; my "chicken cutlets," which are silicone inserts you wear inside your bikini and evening gown; and butt glue, which you use so that the bottom piece of your swimsuit stays in place. I also had hot rollers, a hairbrush and hairspray, jewelry, a swimsuit, two pairs of heels—one six-inch and one three-inch—a bottle of water, Lifesavers, my cell phone, and a few cans of Chocolate Royale SlimFast. Looking at how little I'd brought compared to the other contestants, I couldn't help but feel—no matter how hard I tried—like I could never be the prettiest one, the most prepared one, the best role model. I felt like the mess who didn't bring enough, didn't buy enough, didn't prepare enough, despite all the intense preparation I had done.

My dad said, "Good luck, Ab."

I didn't want him to know how I felt, so I said, "This looks like fun. Thanks so much for letting me do this!" But what I really meant was, "Oh my God, how did I get myself into this?"

I was surrounded by living dolls. These women were flawless from head to toe. Well, this was where I had to force myself to be confident. I thought of the hours in the gym, all the money, time, and heart I had invested in this. I told myself, *This is no time to be scared. I CAN do this! Don't be nervous . . . nervous people don't get very far . . . No matter what, never let them see ya sweat! It's your time to step up to the plate and hit that ball out of the park!*

During prelims, as the girls compete, the judges watch every single step you take. The process is really hard, physically and mentally. It's such a long day and the whole time you have to tell yourself, *I'm not cold . . . I'm not hungry . . . I'm not dying in these shoes.* And you aren't judged only on your appearance. They judge stuff like: Do you make eye contact, are you smiling, are you natural, poised, confident? So you're constantly thinking, *Suck it in, breathe, laugh, think of something clever to say.*

To my surprise, we started the day off by learning the dance number that all the girls would perform at the start of the live show the following night. Dancing is something I never want to do. My first thought was, *I'm disabled . . . I can't dance.* But then, in my mind, I heard Keith saying, "Miss Iowa will do an opening dance."

We danced to Eartha Kitt's rendition of "Santa Baby." There was a kick line and then, as we all walked in a circle formation, a whole bunch of totally contradictory thoughts went tumbling through my head: *I can do it . . . I don't want to do it . . . I'll look different than other people doing it but accomplishment begins with "I'll try," so let's try this dance!*

It only took a moment for these girls to show me their true colors. They were the nicest girls I had ever met.

Pageant girls think of themselves as a community, and no one hesitated in helping me with the dance and letting me hold on to them while we did it. It was so much fun I almost forgot I had CP.

We practiced the dance for a long time and then we practiced walking the runway, which we would have to do that night in front of the audience and the judges. I almost fainted when I saw that runway. It was very high, very narrow, and very scary. There were three Xs marked on it, and at each X we had to pause and turn around. Considering the way I walk, I wasn't sure I could do it. Just for this pageant, I had purchased the tallest high-heeled shoes I had ever worn. They were the six-inch high heels I'd brought, which are some serious heels! And when I put them on and stood up in my bikini on this little wooden runway, I didn't think it would be possible to walk. I was sure I was going to topple right over. I have always had a fear of heights, so it was pretty terrifying to be on a ten-foot-high, narrow runway looking down on dozens of tables where people would be eating dinner. I had a vision of me falling down in the center of a table and people screaming and food and dishes flying all over.

I was lucky that it had been arranged for me to have an escort to hold on to. I was the only contestant who had one, or I should say, I was the only contestant who *had* to have one. When I entered the competition, I had explained to the pageant organizers why I needed an escort. None of the other girls were going to have one, but for me they hired a really nice guy whose wife was a volunteer at the pageant. He wasn't a big guy, but that runway was so narrow that he and I could hardly fit side by side on it without falling off. Also, because he was small, I wasn't sure he could hold me up if I tripped. I told myself I'd been really stupid to come there at all, but since I had, I might as well "run the race and finish well." Anyway, in forty-eight hours it would all be over.

I was starving by the time we broke for dinner, but I decided to hold back when I saw that the pageant committee had ordered us all the foods I love and hadn't eaten for months: spaghetti, bread, butter, cookies, soda. Where were the veggies and protein I had gotten used to? I had worked too hard for too many months, and the judging was just hours away. I told myself, *You can eat giant platefuls of spaghetti for the rest of your life . . . after this weekend.* Though I have to admit, I did break down and eat one cookie.

When I put on my makeup for the evening, I concentrated on my eyes, which are my best feature. The ballroom was decorated with the most beautiful Christmas decorations ever. There were big white hanging snowflakes, fake powdered snow, sparkles everywhere, and dozens of round tables where our families and friends would be sitting.

The prelims show begins with all the girls standing onstage. Then we introduce ourselves; when it got to my turn, I said, "Abbey Curran, twenty, Davenport, Iowa." Everyone clapped, and I could tell where my dad was sitting because he was clapping the loudest. It made me feel so good to be in a moment when he really showed he believed in me!

Then there's the swimsuit portion, which begins with walking that runway. I was number 38, so there were many beautiful girls before me and about twenty girls behind me. I stood in line freezing in my turquoise bikini that I had ever so carefully glued myself into. The swimsuit part of a pageant is always superfrightening to me, since I worry about falling, and falling in a tiny bikini is not a good situation.

But actually, I was excited for swimsuit because people assume the "challenged girl" can't be in fit condition, and I was ready to show them they were wrong. I had spent so many hours in the gym and so many days watching what I ate, and I was excited to show everyone that the "challenged girl" had a six-pack.

When you step onto the runway, the spotlight blinds

you. I took my escort's arm and walked out, making sure I was smiling all the while and making eye contact with the judges. I got to all three *X*s and didn't wobble so much that I was ever in danger of falling off. It seemed to take forever, and when it was over, I was smiling for real. I had made it! I had survived!

After everyone finished on the runway, we had to leave the stage and walk around those circular tables where our families were eating dinner. We walked in a long line, and we had to prance around the people while they ate. Believe me, it takes a lot of guts to be up close and personal with hundreds of strangers when you're wearing a bikini. You've gotta stay poised, look happy, keep smiling, and look great doing it. I smiled, but secretly it was my least favorite part of that whole wonderful night because I was so much slower than any of the girls ahead of me that I made a huge gap in the line.

I couldn't wait to get into that evening gown! I never felt as beautiful as I did when I put on that dress and my six-inch heels. I needed to *own* that runway. Maybe I could. I stood tall and felt pretty. That minute on the runway in my gown was amazing. I forgot about the narrow runway because I felt like I was in heaven, floating on clouds. It was a feeling I never expected.

After we all stepped out in our evening gowns, the

judges picked the top ten—but we wouldn't find out who they were until the next night, at the live pageant. The show would begin with all the girls doing the opening dance number. Then the top ten would be called and the girls who weren't in it would be free to go home. So for the majority of the contestants, the actual pageant would be a very short night.

It was around midnight when prelims ended. I felt I did well, even though I didn't think I could compare to all those other girls. When my parents and Tessa and I were heading back to the hotel, my mother said she wanted to make the three-hour drive back home to get my grandparents and bring them back for the pageant. My grandparents had come to every pageant I ever competed in, but I told her it wouldn't be a good idea to go to the trouble of bringing them along.

"There's no need to go get them," I said. "I'll probably be going home after the opening number."

The next night, an hour before the Miss Iowa pageant was to begin, I slipped into a beautiful Marilyn Monroe type of dress that was superfitted. The pageant had given us strict guidelines for what the dress for the opening number had to look like: a cocktail dress—which meant it had to be short—and it had to be gem-colored, which is why my dress was a deep sapphire blue. I looked at myself in a full-length mirror, from the front and the side, and for the first time ever in my life I loved what I saw.

The dance number went well. It was even fun, and I didn't worry about falling because one of the other girls let me hold on to her. When it ended, we all stood onstage and waited for the names of the girls in the top ten to be called. Out in the audience, I could see my dad, who had cheered so much for me the night before, looking at his watch, probably figuring that I'd be dismissed from the competition in a few minutes and calculating how soon we could get home. That really hurt, even though I myself figured that my time in the pageant was near its end. I could see the families of other contestants holding up banners and signs, and then there was my tiny cheering section who were not cheering at all, and instead looked to me like they were just waiting for it to be over. I understood it, though: The first night they had cheered because despite all the odds against it, I had made it to the pageant. But this was the night when the winner would be crowned, and the idea that I would be the winner, or even make the top ten, seemed impossible to them—and to me.

The names of the first six girls were called. They

were all perfect tens. Then they called a seventh name. It was mine. But I didn't move because sometimes you hear things and don't believe them because what you are hearing is too good to be true. After a few seconds my escort told me we needed to go forward and join the other girls. I was just beside myself. I did it! I had made the top ten!!! Amazing!!!

When you're in the top ten, one of the judges asks you a question that you have to answer onstage. I was hoping my question wouldn't be something like: If you could be any kind of flower, what would you be and why?

But instead their question was, "Why did you decide to compete in this pageant?" What I told them combined my own feelings with the words of Shirley Cothran Barret that had so inspired me: "Every accomplishment, small or great, begins with two words . . . 'I'll try.' We never know unless we try . . . I am not here tonight just for myself, but for everyone else with a challenge who is afraid to try. We might strike out, we might get a home run, or we might only get to first base . . . but we never know unless we try . . . so I am playing ball tonight!"

When I finished there was a lot of clapping. I was surprised by that. It felt really nice.

I honestly can't tell you how I felt about anything that happened next because numbness had set in. There

I was at Miss Iowa USA, aka the NFL of the pageant world, and they called my name for the top five!

Then the judges took one last look at us in evening gowns, and after that there was a little break while they ranked the top five in the order they wanted and determined the Queen.

Finally, they were ready to reveal the winner. As the curtain came up and the snowflakes twinkled, I clenched the arm of my escort. I was walking out onstage at Miss Iowa USA as a top five finalist! A top five finalist! How could this be possible? All I knew was that I couldn't stop smiling, not because I had to, but because I was truly happy. For the first time in my life, I experienced pure happiness.

I stood with the other four girls, who were all stunning and far more gorgeous than I could ever imagine being. Then the emcee started to announce the winners: he called the fourth runner-up . . . third runner-up . . . second runner-up. There were only two of us left: Ali Wright, a radiant blond beauty—and me.

Now the worst case was that I was first runner-up, and that would be extremely amazing! Ali grabbed my hands, and I remember looking right at her. She had huge dimples, beautiful skin . . . everything about her was flawless. She was calm and poised and her bright ocean-blue eyes sparkled. I had always wished mine did that.

I'm not sure why I was shaking, because I knew I wasn't going to win. I guess I was still excited and not believing I was in the top two. I started talking to her. Talking always helps me calm down; I can't stand silence. So I told her how proud I was of her and how I couldn't believe we were there. I kept saying, "You've got this, you've got this . . . I'll come to Miss USA and cheer for you."

Then I heard the words: ". . . and the first runner-up is . . . Ali Wright!" My legs buckled beneath me. I nearly dropped to the floor. No way! No way! I clasped my hand over my mouth. I felt hot tears stinging my eyes. And then there it was, coming loud and clear through the microphone: "Your 2008 Miss Iowa USA is Abbey Curran."

I didn't believe what was happening to me. I'm not just saying that to be cheesy; it's true. It's like I was watching myself from afar . . . wondering, *How can this be?* If you ask my parents for pictures of this, they don't have any because they could not believe what they were seeing. They sat frozen as I stood frozen.

That was the moment . . . my moment. It was the

moment that changed my life, and I think it also changed a tiny bit of the world, because this wasn't a win only for me. It was a win for everyone born with a disability or a challenge. It was a win that had an impact on the glass ceiling that keeps us down, that makes us feel like outsiders, that leaves us feeling inferior. Now, there was a great big crack in that glass ceiling.

As they crowned me, I stood on that stage knowing I almost hadn't entered the pageant because of my CP. All I could do was be grateful that I had found the strength and the encouragement to follow my dream.

I remember every single moment of that night. It was as if all the stars in the sky were shining just so I could wish on them. Winning that crown meant the world to me. I didn't know it then, but I would get my first kiss thanks to that crown, I would finally have a date thanks to that crown, I would make new friends thanks to that crown. I have the confidence to get out of bed each day because of that crown and—on the downside—I have a lot of credit card debt thanks to that crown.

The November day that I became Miss Iowa was like my birthday—it felt like the day I was really born. I slept in the crown all night. It was very uncomfortable but I would not take it off.

Much later, someone asked me if I would sell my crown, and I told them I couldn't sell it even for a million dollars because it's my oxygen tank. That crown was an answer to my prayers. It has given me hope, given me faith and courage.

Up to that night, I had attempted a lot and managed to win exactly one thing—the Miss World Festival. That was it, unless you want to count the cups I got for the pony contests my grandpa rigged for me. Other than that: twenty years of zip! Search my name on the internet—you'll see! No sports, no essay prizes or business awards.

After I was crowned Miss Iowa, people didn't know me just as Abbey, the girl who walks weird. Now it was people bragging that "MISS IOWA USA is in my class! Abbey Curran!" That crown meant that people remembered me for something other than being disabled.

Winning Miss Iowa and changing the pageant world a bit made me the happiest and the proudest I have ever been. I know that some people felt sorry for me and thought I had won only because I was disabled. I wondered about that, too. I've thought about it a lot, but because I have some faith in myself now, I don't believe it's the reason I won.

Even today it makes me cry just thinking about the moment I was crowned. It was the moment I stopped being a joke and became a "somebody." Not forever, because nothing is forever. But for a while.

Riding my pony, Shadow, a present from my grandpa Jack. Shadow and I won the prettiest pony prize in the Sheffield Homecoming Parade, my first trophy ever! If you look closely, you can see that I am wearing a tiara.

Celebrating my birthday with Grandma Wink.

Christmas, age 9.

Senior year of high school. Kewanee, Illinois.

Competing in the Miss Dream Girls USA pageant in Chicago. It was my third pageant ever, and I walked away as Miss Dream Girls USA Spokesmodel Queen.

In the Geneseo, Illinois, parade as Miss World Festival. My friend Jan Sellman drove me in her car.

After emceeing an event at the Beverly Hills Hotel for Looking Beyond, an organization that helps special-needs kids. I got to meet—and kiss!—Rick Hoyt. He was being honored along with his dad, Dick. Rick has cerebral palsy; his dad pushes and pulls him through triathlons. They've competed in six Ironman triathlons and seventy-two marathons!

At an event for the Miss USA Pageant in Las Vegas with my friends Chelsey Sophia Rodgers (Miss District of Columbia USA), Vincenza Carrieri-Russo (Miss Delaware USA), and Brittany Mason (Miss Indiana USA).

The evening gown competition at the Miss USA pageant! I was escorted by Rocky Fain.

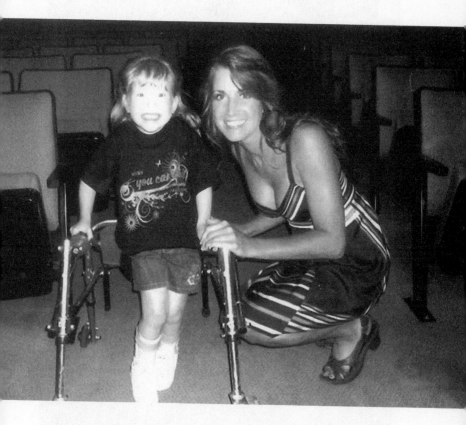

With one of the Miss You Can Do It contestants. Their courage inspires me every day. I am so proud of them!

Back home on the farm. I still love horses!

ELEVEN
Miss Iowa

efore I went to the Miss Iowa contest, I was sitting in my dorm room waiting for life to happen. I had been like a caterpillar, yearning to be a butterfly, wondering if I would ever evolve into something more, something better than what I was at the time.

Back then, I would wish on the moon every night. Of course, I still prayed, but wishing is different than praying. A prayer is something you say to God; a wish is something you whisper to your own heart. I love wishing on the moon. I think people take the moon for granted. It's the biggest, most beautiful thing in the sky, and people don't take the time to wish on it. Well, I have always wished on the moon. I'd wish to be beautiful, to be successful. I'd wish to find my way in life, and of course I'd wish to be loved.

Just as I had my wishes, I still had my dreams, which at that time were mostly focused on things I could do to make life better for the people I loved the most: I could buy my grandma a new home; I could buy my dad a new tractor so he doesn't have to get upset because he has to keep repairing his old one; I could buy new carpet for our basement so when it floods my mom won't be frustrated and sad. I could hire a twenty-four-hour-a-day companion for my ninety-one-year-old friend and buy a wheelchair van for my Miss You Can Do It contestants. I could donate money to amazing doctors like my ob-gyn who, by assuring me that I can definitely have babies, gave me peace of mind and changed my life, and I know she could do the same for other women with disabilities if only I could bring them together. Another thing I dreamed of doing was making sure that everyone in the Kewanee nursing home received beautiful flowers on Christmas and Valentine's Day.

When I told these dreams to other people, they would roll their eyes or even laugh. But after I won Miss Iowa, I wasn't the dreaming dork anymore—not to my family or my friends. Suddenly, for the first time ever, I was *it*! I would think back to all those times when I felt so bad because no one wanted to help me or invite me to a party. But it was all worth it, because the sadness then made the happiness now even greater. I was finally wanted, admired, and appreciated. People I didn't even know would stop me on the street to say congratulations and to ask what being in a pageant was really like. They looked at me in a way that no one had looked at me before. Before, when I was talking about something good that had happened to me, people would look at me as if they didn't believe a word I said. Now they nodded and smiled as I talked, and made me feel that they really were interested in what I was saying. Believe me, that was a first.

It made me feel on top of the world, even though there were still a lot of doubters and haters who said I won Miss Iowa only because I have CP. One person said, "Did anyone else compete in the pageant besides you?" It was supposed to be a joke, but it was still hurtful.

When I was in grade school, I spent a lot of time perfecting my signature just in case I ever had to sign an autograph someday. I'd write *Abbey Curran* over and over and try to decide if cursive was better than print and just how many curls I wanted to put into my *C*. The other kids would laugh and ask why I was bothering with a perfect signature since I'd never need it. But finally, I was right! All of that practice came in handy when I started signing lots of autographs.

One of my first appearances was at the Iowa State Fair. My best friend and college roommate Sarah went with me. She was proud of me for becoming Miss Iowa, but because we'd been friends way before that and lived in the same room at school, to her I was still just her room-mate Abbey—the girl who liked staying up late with her and who always gets messy and sweaty when she walks to class.

But on that day I wasn't messy. I was wearing a beau-tiful strapless cotton dress patterned with roses, plus my white satin pageant sash that's lined on each side with dozens of little crystals that look like diamonds. Topping it all off was my Miss Iowa crown. As soon as we walked through the entry gate all sorts of people came toward me: there were older ladies with bluish-white hair, and young girls, and a lot of young boys who were totally embarrassed because their parents were shoving them toward me so I could kiss their cheek and leave a lipstick mark on it. The girls and the older ladies were hugging me, asking for pictures, autographs, and kisses. Sarah couldn't believe it. She had been supportive of me when I entered the Miss Iowa competition, but I don't think that she ever in a million years believed I could win. And as she watched all these people swarming around me, she was laughing so hard, and she was like, "Really?" It was the first time she had seen how my life had changed, and once she got over her surprise, she was really happy for me.

There were so many people around me that I couldn't have gotten away even if I had wanted to, which I didn't. No one noticed that I had a challenge except a very few who knew it because they had challenges themselves. I felt wonderful! It was amazing to have people love you and admire you and talk about you in a good way. I had never even dreamed of having anything like it. For weeks and months afterward, I would head into the local Walmart for tampons or cat food or something spectacular like that and people would come over to me and want to talk, and they'd listen really closely to every word I said. But why? What did I do differently? Before Miss Iowa, I worked out just like I always did, I ate very carefully, just like I always did, and I had hope, just like I always do. What made me a "somebody," what got me unstuck, was that somebody had placed a shiny piece of metal on my head and given me a new name—"Miss Iowa."

Don't get me wrong—it definitely was a dream come true, and I was thrilled. But I was also amazed to discover how much this new name turned my world upside down and changed how people saw me, how they treated me, how they respected me. And what's bizarre is that the people you think will be most affected by your newfound fame aren't affected by it at all, and the people who do care about it are the ones who you'd figure couldn't care less. The people who cared about it—besides my own family—were people I had never met until after the pageant, the people who came up to me at the Iowa State Fair or at Walmart or on Main Street or wherever. Honestly, I can't imagine why my being Miss Iowa meant so much to them, but it did.

The people who didn't care were the very ones I would have loved to impress: the cool guys and the cool girls at school. But no matter what I did, they knew they were still way cooler than me, and frankly, I knew it, too. I really wasn't any different than I'd ever been. I mean, for example, not long after I became Miss Iowa, I went to a speaking engagement in Baton Rouge, Louisiana, with my friend Sam. I've known her since kindergarten, and she is so much cooler than me, it isn't even funny. The event I was there for was designed to benefit children with disabilities and was billed as "Developing Dreams with Miss Iowa." I was all dressed up and wearing my crown and sash, and when we got off the elevator, the guy who booked me for this event and paid for us both to fly down to Baton Rouge, was waiting for us across the lobby. I pointed him out to Sam.

So (like normal girls do) Sam swishes her butt and clicks her heels and heads over to say hello to him. But she let go of my arm, so as I carefully tried to walk across the lobby, I went smack down, like a small earthquake shaking the ground, and my crown fell off and rolled away while I just lay there. Well, nothing makes you feel like a bigger loser than that. I remember crying in our hotel room that night and telling her how hurt I was that she had let go of me. She said, "You can walk by yourself, Abbey." Which is true, but I look awful when I'm doing it, and I start to sweat, and I worry about falling down. Let's face it: The only reason I was allowed to have someone travel with me was so they could help me. And I couldn't help thinking that if she had been a better friend, she would have understood how much I needed her help at moments like that, and how bad I felt when she let go of my arm to click off to meet the man who had booked *me*, not her. So once again, I felt like a huge loser . . . only now I was a loser with a crown. By the way, it wasn't the last time I fell smack on my face when I was wearing that crown. You can actually count the number of times I fell because every single fall is represented by a rhinestone missing from my crown.

Sam and I still did things together after that, but it was never the same, which made me sad. Until that incident in Baton Rouge, I thought she was one of the best friends I ever had.

With or without my crown, I realized that cool people would still never think I was as cool as them. Which was fair, because I wasn't. I would never be the one they would ask for advice or learn anything from. Well, it finally occurred to me that true friends see each other as equals; you're as good as them and they're as good as you. You don't have to look up to each other, and you'd never look down. Part of my growing-up process was starting to understand that these "cool" people weren't my friends at all.

I think the people who cared the most about my being Miss Iowa were my aunts and uncles and cousins. When I walked into my grandmother's house for Christmas dinner, everybody was really excited to talk to me. That was a shock, because in twenty-one years, it had never happened. Before, I would walk in and get asked pleasant questions like, "Do you have a job yet?" "How long do you plan to be in school?" "Still living in a 'dream world'?" "How long do you plan on doing this pageant thing [aka Miss You Can Do It]?" "Do you still watch *SpongeBob*?" As far as that last annoying question goes, I would always tell them, "Yes, of course I watch *SpongeBob*! It's one of my favorite shows!" And then they would give me a look that said they thought I was crazy.

But now, they wanted autographed pictures for their friends, and they had millions of questions. They wanted to know about life as Miss Iowa. It was amazing. They asked me, "What was it like to meet Donald Trump?" "Where are you traveling to next?" "What is Sherri Hill's dress shop like?" "Did you get to meet her?" "What do you do to get such pretty skin?" The other thing that happened is that people suddenly stuck up for me. For instance, if one of my mother's friends asked, "Are you still watching *SpongeBob*?" in that nasty way people often had when they asked me things, then my mother or grandmother would say, "Yes, it relaxes her. You'd understand if you saw her travel schedule last week. I don't know how she manages it all. I'd be so stressed if I was her."

Winning Miss Iowa meant I was going to compete in the Miss USA pageant, which is broadcast on national TV and is a really big deal. I could hardly believe that I would be one of the contestants, girls who represent each of the fifty states plus one more who represents the District of Columbia.

Soon after I was crowned, the head of the Miss Iowa organization told my parents, "This is the big leagues. It's a once-in-a-lifetime experience, and it takes a lot of time and money, but only fifty-one women in the country get to do this each year, and she will never get this opportunity again."

It truly was the "big leagues," and it was also a great big expense. And my parents were fine with that! I was Miss Iowa now, and only the best for Miss Iowa. They liked the idea that, after all the things I'd been through because of CP, I was now a "beauty queen." Not to mention the fact that I had made history. Suddenly, my father and grandmother gave me endless amounts of money. Before, investing in me was about as good a bet as investing in a racehorse with a broken leg, and it felt like I had to beg for every last nickel. Now, my family's attitude was: The sky's the limit. Things like an evening dress that I'd had to beg and bargain for became a given. If I said I needed a new gown, nobody blinked an eye. It used to be that everyone thought buying a thousand-dollar gown for me was a ridiculous waste of money, but now with Miss USA on the horizon, my parents began to think that if I had a really gorgeous gown, my chances of winning would be better, which was true. So now it was, "If Abbey needs a gown, let's hop on a plane, fly halfway across the country to Oklahoma City, and get it."

The reason we had to fly to OKC is that it's where Serendipity is. Serendipity is a huge, unbelievably beautiful store where there are rows and rows of the most magical gowns you've ever seen. Naturally, the store is owned by Sherri Hill and her daughter Kara, and it's where all the pageant girls go when they're competing in the most important pageants. For Miss Iowa, it was fine that I wore a copy of the fantastic Sherri Hill dress that has been designed for a former Miss America. But competing in Miss USA was like playing in the Super Bowl, you had to have the right uniform, and the only way to get that was to have Sherri Hill design a dress for you and make it to order. These dresses are really pricey—seven or eight thousand dollars each—and what you're paying for is the very best design for your particular body. You tell Sherri what you want, she sketches out a few designs, and you discuss them with her and then pick one. I adore AB crystals and my gown was supposed to have dozens and dozens of them on the bodice, but when I flew back to OKC to get the dress fitted, I decided there weren't enough crystals and she added more.

Working with Sherri Hill on my dress was a wonderful experience I will always remember. She made me feel like a princess with a fairy godmother who wanted to make everything absolutely perfect.

I soon discovered that if you win a big pageant, there are a lot of perks that go along with it. For instance, I went on vacation to Disneyland not long after I won the title. My friend and I were waiting in the longest lines for hours until my friend told a manager that I was Miss Iowa, and suddenly we were taken to the front of every line. At the Iowa State Fair, I was given anything I wanted to eat for free. Soderstrom gave me free facials and treatments and even more pampering than they'd given me before. I'm not sure why everyone makes such a big fuss about pageant girls, since most people think we're all about looks and not much else. In truth, all of the pageant girls I've met are amazing people, but they're not judged on that. They're not judged on community service or school grades or kindness or how much they care about others. It's just evening gowns and swimsuits and a little speech or answering a question onstage. Yet, even though the special treatment kind of mystified me, I also learned that it makes you feel better about yourself. It makes you feel that people are interested in you, that they want to please you, and somehow that makes you a nicer and happier person. When you are the reigning Miss Iowa and your name is on the news and your pictures are in the paper, people want to help you partly to be nice, but also so they can tell other people they helped you. A store or an office will stay open and wait for you; people are friendly and say, "Hey, let me help you walk; aren't you Miss Iowa?"

But I never forgot that Miss Iowa is just a title, even if it was the best title of my life and I had never been so proud. It was important to me to remember that, in the grand scheme of things, it's just a job description, like doctor, lawyer, bus driver, or plumber.

My job was to represent the great state of Iowa at all sorts of events, and I loved it. I went to ribbon cuttings and grand openings. Some days I'd drive five hours to a grand opening, stay there for two hours, and then have a five-hour drive home. But I didn't mind. I went to the Iowa State Fair, but also to camps for kids, to colleges, and to events at Iowa State University like wheelchair basketball (aka the hardest game ever . . . I tried it).

I went to many schools and spoke about bullying. I went to banquets, dinners, church events, nursing homes. One day, I drove three hours each way to a nursing home that was having a Valentine's Day party, and I took my grandma Wink with me. I spoke for about ten minutes about how much I love my grandparents.

Some of those sweet residents don't ever have anyone to visit with them, and it was an honor for me to sit with them, hold their hands, and tell them how happy I was to be there for them, even though it was only for such a short time. I remember kissing the cheek of a ninety-year-old man at one nursing home I visited. He cried, and it touched my heart. Things like that make you realize just how many people need you, and frankly, even though that made me feel good, it also made me feel bad—because I couldn't be in every city and town every day, and when it came to some of the events that are far away, I knew I probably wouldn't have time to go back. I have to hope that, since my visits got written up in the local newspaper, it would remind others how important it is to spend time with the forgotten people in nursing homes.

I also became a keynote speaker at events all around the country. I wanted to inspire other women to follow their dreams, and the speeches I gave included some of the incredibly wise and uplifting things I'd learned from the people who had inspired me, especially my trainer, Keith, and Shirley Barret. One part of my speeches went like this: "Everyone has challenges in life that you have to overcome. You have to do it with a positive attitude and a lot of persistence.

Every accomplishment, be it small or great, begins with two words: 'I'LL TRY!' You never know unless you try. All of us build walls, so to speak, in our own heads, and those walls keep us from being everything we can possibly be. We build walls that sometimes set us up for failure. There are also walls that other people have built around us. We have to pull those walls down. I believe that the main ingredient necessary to being a winner is refusing to be held back from a dream."

One of the surprising things about winning Miss Iowa was that, about an hour after I won, people from all over the country were commenting about it. Some of the comments were good, some were bad, some made me cry, and some filled me with confidence. There were also a few that make me physically sick.

The ones that bothered me the most were from people who said that, according to the Miss USA rules, every girl is required to walk onstage alone, so "How would this Miss Iowa get to compete in Miss USA since she needs an escort?" That stressed me out. I had to find out if it was true, but since I won on a Saturday night, I had to wait until Monday. I kept thinking how weird and awful and embarrassing it would be if I had come this far for nothing.

Luckily, my fear only lasted a few days, since the people in the Trump Organization—which runs the pageant—soon learned who I was and that I had a disability. Someone from the organization emailed me to say I'd be getting a call from them, which made me a little nervous, to put it mildly. All I could think was, *They have to let me compete in this pageant.* So many things ran through my mind. What if they take back my title? What if they tell me I can compete in their pageant but only if I can walk on my own? What if they tell me that I should never have been allowed to compete for Miss Iowa to begin with? No matter what, I knew that I would not allow my CP to hold me back. I would crawl across that stage if I had to because there was no way I was giving up that moment.

Finally, I got the call. And boy, was I pleasantly surprised. They were some of the nicest people I have ever dealt with, and they kept making sure I had everything I needed! From then on, I'd get emails galore and call after call. "What about the airport, Abbey? Do you need someone to help you to security?" Their willingness to help me was a huge and unexpected relief. They were so kind and made it so easy for me that it left me wondering why people can't be nice all the time, not just to me, but to anyone, whether they happened to be physically challenged or not.

Being in the Miss USA competition was bigger than anything I had ever done; it was bigger than anything I had dreamed. And—in spite of my nerves, in spite of the doubters—I knew for sure that, come hell or high water, I was going.

TWELVE
The Big One

The Miss USA pageant was held in April, five months after I became Miss Iowa. As the date of the pageant came nearer, the online gossip about me ramped up again and was worse than ever. Men were posting horrid comments. A lot of people posted stuff like, "I guess anyone can win Miss Iowa." And then there were the ones who wrote that I wouldn't have the courage to show up at the pageant.

I was so angry and upset reading these nasty things written by people who had never even met me. It was scary that so many strangers had such terrible feelings about me. For a few days right before the pageant, I had this awful picture of me limping across the stage in my high heels and my blue bikini, while people in the audience sat there laughing. It still makes me a little ill that random people can be so mean, especially when they've never been to Miss USA, and probably never even competed in a pageant.

One good thing happened from those nasty remarks, though. I printed them out, took them to the gym, and read them with Keith, whose attitude about them was, "So what? Who cares?" That made me feel a whole lot better, and from then on, whenever I read one of those awful comments, I got so motivated to prove them wrong that all of a sudden I could lift bigger weights, do more crunches, and run even faster on the StairMaster. And Keith was the best. He's a one-in-a-million guy, that's for sure. He never doubted me, and he made me feel so wonderful when I was working with him because he would smile with so much pride at how all of his hard work with me was paying off.

In his gym, I was surrounded by past and present fair queens, girls who either were or had been Miss Henry County or Miss World Festival. They were all jogging and looking flawless and even though I had won a bigger title than they had, they were still the kind of girls I strived to be like. They moved as gracefully and easily as athletes, and I envied that. For me to do workouts similar to the ones they did, I needed physical help. That meant that Keith would have to hold on to my waist so I could do leg workouts or bend over and not fall. Sometimes I'd get kind of shaky and nearly hit the floor, but he would always catch me.

When Keith started working with me, I had no developed muscles, and now I had that six-pack I'd been so proud to show off on the runway at the Miss Iowa competition. I about died getting it, but I was so lucky to have Keith because he didn't let me quit. He'd plan out my meals for me and was very supportive. He'd always said, "Come on, you can do it, you've got this, Miss Iowa."

The few times I wanted to miss a session he would say, "Come on, Abbey . . . don't be slacking, get in here." And I always did.

Keith is one of the people who taught me how to be positive about myself. He wanted me to tell myself, *Yes, I walk different and yes, I do have a disability, BUT that doesn't mean I can't score the highest in swimsuit and be the hottest, fittest woman in the entire competition.*

The day I was supposed to leave for the Miss USA pageant, I woke up sick. Maybe it was just a big case of cold feet, but whatever it was, I had a fever. My bedding was dripping with sweat, I had chills, and I was nauseated. I had never felt that awful before. I was about to set off for Las Vegas, where the pageant would be held and where I—and all the other contestants—would spend the entire three weeks leading up to the event.

My biggest fear was that I would be away from my basic support system. A thousand negative thoughts were racing through my mind: *In Las Vegas there will be no comforting grandmas, no kittens to cuddle, nowhere to hide. I won't be able to run to my room and lock the door. There is no backing out. I will be surrounded by the most gorgeous women in the world. What will they think of me? Will they think I belong there? I hope they are nice. I wonder if anyone will help me walk. Will they understand that I don't like asking for help, and will they resent me for needing it?*

The other thing I thought was: *Now I have to go and walk and walk and walk in front of the world.* That was the worst of it. The very thought was just terrifying to me. So going to the Miss USA pageant turned out to be a dream and a nightmare wrapped up into one.

Luckily, I have always believed in the power of positive thinking, so I told myself I had to get over feeling sick, and I did. The next step was to get on a plane and fly to Dallas to get a connecting flight to Las Vegas. It was during a layover in the Dallas airport that I first spotted one of the other contestants. As I would find out, her name was Leah, and she was so gorgeous I nearly fell over.

I don't think I'll ever forget that first sighting: her perfectly curled, long, thick, dark hair, her fake eyelashes highlighting her huge brown eyes, her French manicure and gorgeous fuchsia dress—the prettiest cocktail dress I have ever seen in my entire life.

She was as lovely and delicate as a porcelain doll right out of the box. I had never seen anyone so flawless.

How could I ever hope to compete in the same pageant as a girl like that? I needed soooo much more work. I wasn't prepared. For all the careful planning and preparing I had done, it just hadn't occurred to me to get hair and lash extensions or a better manicure or more of a spray tan. *Dang it*, I thought, *maybe I should have looked into these things a little more.*

I had worn what I thought was a good outfit for the occasion: a cute black-and-white top with white pants and black sandals. I had figured it would be the exact right thing for traveling all day, but now I felt so underdressed, so wrong. Leah looked like a girl who was ready to walk out onstage in a beauty competition. I looked like I'd come from some town in the Midwest no one had ever heard of. But that's me: the hog farmer's daughter. It would never have occurred to me to wear a cocktail dress on my way to the Miss USA competition. I thought, *Why do I always think of the great ideas after it's too late?*

Seeing Leah definitely expanded my idea of beauty. I had thought my classmates were so beautiful—and they are—but they don't hold a candle to Leah's stunning elegance and poise and composure. The difference between Leah and the girls I knew at home was the difference between going to the county fair or going to Disney World. Both are fun, but only one is the very best.

Leah was Miss Mississippi and she absolutely intimidated me, but I had to suck it up, and I tried to act as if I thought I was on her level. Sometimes you have to push yourself to seem confident, so I stood as tall as I could, forced myself to smile, and went over and started talking to her. I wasn't surprised when she told me her full name was Leah Laviano; of course she would have a beautiful name. She was supernice, and we agreed we'd sit next to each other on the plane from Dallas to Las Vegas, but to do that I needed to switch seats with an old man whose seat was next to Leah's. He was staring at her so hard it looked like his eyes were going to pop out of his head. So naturally, he refused to change seats with me.

After meeting Leah, I realized that I was totally unprepared for the next three weeks. I had packed a couple of sundresses . . . wrong! And jean shorts with cute tops . . . double wrong! *Seriously, Abbey*, I thought, *that's what you do in Kewanee, not in Las Vegas with the Miss USA contestants.*

The thing is, I didn't even own anything as glamorous as Leah's cocktail dress. I just wished I had packed better everyday clothes, more jewelry, and nicer shoes. Of course I had my pageant clothes, but that was for competition. I hadn't brought any stunning attire for daytime like the other girls had. I should have known better, and I would have if only I had gone to the pageant training day that my state pageant's directors had designed specifically to prepare me and the girl competing for Miss Teen USA for our competitions. The other girl went, but I didn't want to go, and at the time, I didn't feel the least bit bad about that. I didn't want to hear their ideas about my hair and my nails and my bikini and my clothes. I remember reading the email they sent and thinking, *I don't need this.* Well, I did need it! I really did!

One of the very first things I learned at Miss USA was that even when you've made a stupid wardrobe decision, you have to be confident, so confident that you can convince yourself that everyone else is lame for wearing cocktail dresses to the pool. You need to think you are in the right and they are in the wrong. You need to believe: I am so cool; my jeans are the way to go. I attempted that . . . and I still need to work on it, but it's definitely the thing to do. Instead of being afraid of what the other girls were thinking, I would tell myself that maybe they were wishing they had my outfit. I highly doubted it, but who knows?

Anyway, when we landed in Las Vegas, there were limousines waiting for us. I had never been in a limo before. It was very exciting. There were camera crews everywhere and lots of people from every state who had come to Las Vegas for the shows and the gambling and had decided to spend that afternoon greeting the pageant competitors as they arrived. There would be an announcement each time a contestant got off a plane and then people would start screaming for you and shouting, "Iowa! Hi, Iowa! I'm from Des Moines!" or whatever. It was loud and raucous, but it made me feel really special.

Writing about it makes me tear up a little even now. I had wished and dreamed and prayed just to be somebody. Just to get asked to spend the night at the cool girl's house, to go to a party with the popular group. And even though that never happened, there I was in a limousine with Leah Laviano who—if she had gone to my school—would have been the coolest girl of all time.

We drove down the Las Vegas strip and it all seemed surreal. There were millions of flashing lights and humongous hotels as big and fancy as palaces. The driver took us to a secret underground entrance of the Planet Hollywood Las Vegas Resort and Casino, where we'd all be staying throughout the three weeks of preparations for the pageant and during the event itself. It was thrilling to be in such a ravishing hotel, not because it was so grand and amazing, but because it was the official hotel of the Miss USA pageant and I was there to compete in it!

The hotel was like something right out of a movie, with flakes of what looked like real gold in the granite floors, and everything seeming to sparkle and shimmer. It was very cold, and the cold made everything seem even more dreamlike. In the lobby there was a beautiful desk where we checked in.

Unfortunately, being the farmer's daughter from a tiny town, I didn't have thousands of dollars on me. Not that the other girls did, either—we weren't there because we were rich—but I think all of them were better prepared than me. Little did I know that I needed to pay right away for the entire three weeks at the hotel—well, it goes on your credit card, but in the end the pageant pays you back for it. And sure enough, Miss Iowa's credit card was denied. When they told me, I said, "Oh, try it again!" but I knew my pearly whites were what was filling up that baby. I did have a little credit left on it, just not the thousands needed to pay for the hotel for three weeks, which was the problem. They were nice enough and said I could fix it later, and I remember being so embarrassed when I had to call my parents and get them to take care of it for me. I believe my mom called and gave them her credit card. I felt like an idiot. I would have come prepared if I had known. Note to self: If you ever get to return to Miss USA, read all the instructions they send you and bring money, lashes, hair extensions, and stunning outfits . . . leave the jeans at home.

Eventually it all got squared away and I went upstairs, where I met my room mother, who would be staying in a connecting room to mine. I would soon learn that the pageant was very protective of its girls; for example, there was so much security surrounding us that if we used a public bathroom in a hotel lobby we had to be accompanied there either by our room mother or even someone from the police department. They're so careful, in fact, that when my parents sent me a package, I didn't get it for four days after it arrived because everything we were sent had to first be checked out by the police and then by the bomb-detecting dogs!

* * *

My room mother was named Evett. She was in her late fifties, very pretty, and supersweet—such a happy person all the time, and so helpful. Actually, she was so helpful that she tried to be overly helpful. I mean, it's true that I need help when I'm walking. But the rest of the time I am totally like anyone else. Poor Evett was trying to be so nice, but in the beginning she would offer to do all kinds of things for me that weren't necessary. I'd tell her, "I am pretty sure I don't need assistance putting on my own underpants and swimsuit bottoms!" But after a few days she understood. Part of what made the experience so wonderful is that there were kind people like Evett there. My roommate was Miss Delaware. Her name is Vincenza Carrieri-Russo and she was, and is, absolutely flawless and stunning! She was another girl who made me really nervous. She'd brought boxes and boxes of shoes and clothes and spray-tan stuff and even had a juicer shipped to our room ahead of time. All of my stuff was packed into two old suitcases and I never even dreamed of bringing all the things she had brought. I mean, twenty-five pairs of shoes! I had four pairs with me: one for swimsuit, one for evening gown, and two pairs for those sundresses I had planned to wear on our sightseeing trips.

On that first day we went right to work—dress

fittings, hair, makeup, rehearsals, photos. Even though I felt like the ugly duckling surrounded by some of the most beautiful women in the country, it was still totally AWESOME!

THIRTEEN
A Magical Experience

I
t's no secret that a lot of people think pageant girls are stupid. But I had been in a lot of competitions by then, and the girls in the Miss USA pageant were typical of all the pageant girls I've known. They were very smart: they were nurses, medical students, special education teachers, personal trainers, journalists, college students. Sometimes I get asked if it surprised me to learn that the other contestants were successful academically. I always say, "No, it didn't surprise me because I was doing well in school, too."

Another thing a lot of people think is that so-called beauty queens are lazy and coddled and just sit around getting mani-pedis all the time. The truth is, Miss USA was three weeks of long, hard days. We would wake up about 6:00 a.m. and go to bed around midnight. There were lots of public appearances and signing autographs, but the main part of the day was spent in long rehearsals for the pageant itself—which meant walking, walking, and more walking. In fact, there was so much walking that we had a walking coach. Her name was Lou, and in a way she was like a cheerleader for all the girls. One of the first things she told us was: "There are two types of people in this world: those who want to be you and those who want to marry you."

Lou taught us the "pageant strut," which we did in a huge ballroom in front of mirrors. I watched all these beautiful girls doing that strut and when it was my turn I was supposed to walk in front of them. There was no way I could walk the way those girls walked, but Lou walks with you and cheerleads you the entire time you're walking. So the music is loud and on top of that Lou is screaming so loud that I barely managed to hear what she was saying: "Miss Iowa, you are the hottest woman on this stage . . . Those other girls are just background for you . . . You've got this . . . You will be Miss USA . . . You are so beautiful . . . Everyone wants to be you . . ."

She force-fed me confidence! Whatever I did at the pageant—and long after it—I'd hear Lou's voice in my head screaming *You are the hottest!* And her words helped even though I didn't really believe them. No one had ever said I was hot before, and if they ever did, they certainly wouldn't say it while I was walking!

Before the Miss USA pageant, I had begun to get a lot of requests to do interviews. I was really amazed and happy about this, because it meant that my story was meaningful and worthwhile since it shows that a disabled person can do all sorts of things you might never think they could.

Once I got to Las Vegas, I was interviewed by reporters from *Access Hollywood* and *Inside Edition*. I thought I was just one of the fifty-one contestants being featured in the stories, but they turned out to be all about me. When I saw them, I wasn't too excited, because to tell you the truth, I didn't know that *Inside Edition* or *Access Hollywood* were TV shows. Then I found out that both shows are a big deal and I was really excited. Best of all, one of the reporters quoted me as saying exactly what I wanted everyone to know: "I hope America doesn't see a girl who walks differently. I hope they see someone who can compete like anyone else."

Every one of the Miss USA contestants had left her family and friends behind. We were not allowed to have physical contact with anyone outside the Miss USA Organization.

So if you wanted your back spray-tanned or wanted to borrow shoes or make sure you had curls in the back of your head, you had to make friends. I ended up making great friends. Who would assume that the most beautiful women in the country were also the nicest? We had a blast. It was like three weeks of those supercool high school slumber parties I never got invited to.

These ladies at Miss USA didn't leave me breathless only because of their outer beauty and flawlessness; the other things that knocked me out were their confidence and personality. They were so smart and genuine, and I think that's why the Miss USA pageant is so well-known and watched. These women could be future leaders of our country; any one of them could be the doctor who cures cancer or the business tycoon who saves the economy, *and* in addition to being gorgeous, they are supercaring and friendly. So few people have all those wonderful qualities, and there I was, in rooms that were filled with them!

I didn't feel like the prettiest or most prepared one at Miss USA, but I did feel loved in that great, unconditional way my grandparents have always loved me. All of those amazing women were so nice to me and included me in their groups, and I think I was happier there than I had ever been. The most amazing part was that they kept telling me I was one of them. It was hard for me to believe, but I can't deny that I was accepted as one of them, and I was really surprised when they would take turns letting me hold on to them. No one made me feel bad about myself. I wasn't the outcast. I was fun!

We had the same interests. They were able to understand things my other friends couldn't, like how much a Sherri Hill gown means to you—how it's not just a dress, it's an experience. They knew how many calories are really in a hamburger or a chef's salad. And they knew how hard it was for me to give up my favorite mint chocolate chip ice cream, and understood why I kept saying, "Win or lose, there's a sundae waiting for me after this!"

My new friends understood that it doesn't matter how silly you think a question is; the point is how you handle yourself when you answer it. They could understand that even though pickles are zero calories, if you eat a jar full of them you will swell up like a balloon because there is so much salt in them. And they understood that if there is something about your body you don't like, it's okay to work toward changing it. It's also completely okay to not change anything about yourself. The point is to discover what makes you happy, and then act on what you've learned. Happy people make other people happy.

It may seem shallow to you, but I am happier because when I didn't like the way my teeth looked, I got veneers. Because of them, I smile more at others even if they aren't smiling at me. I am happy and want to show it. When I am happy, I'm not thinking about myself, so I can focus more on why others aren't happy and try to do something about it. I might not have the confidence to reach out in those ways if it weren't for those outer improvements. And it's not just because of the way they make me look. It's also because I believe it is important to do all you can to be your best, and that includes everything from reading good books to getting enough exercise and sleep to doing good deeds. My Miss USA friends understand that. And we also understand that what matters most is the way people are on the inside.

You'd think that at a competition we wouldn't be friends, but we laughed together and cried together and we felt we had bonded for life because we were all living the same dream.

One of the girls at Miss USA was a supermodel who did fashion shows for many of the top designers. Her name was Casandra Tressler. She was Miss Maryland and she was six feet tall and superslim, with long blond hair.

One night, sitting on the bus on the way to one of our

events in Las Vegas, she grabbed my arm and said, "Sit by me." What?! Me? Sit by her?! In the past I was lucky if I could sneak my way into a seat at the cool table at lunch in high school. But none of those girls ever said, "Abbey, I want to sit by you."

I was shocked that someone so cool wanted to be my friend, and it turned out she was a true friend. We hung out together a lot in Vegas, and since she packed about ten bottles of this really great spray-tan stuff, she was nice enough to give me one. I sat with Cassie on the way to the opening of a restaurant called Sedona and we got to try it out first. As soon as we sat down at our table, the owner of the restaurant sat with us—she was Rachel Smith, Miss USA 2007. I couldn't believe it. Me, Abbey Curran, who grew up on a farm with the hogs and was never cool, sitting at a table with a Miss USA and a runway model! Cassie and I have stayed in contact. She has come to my Miss You Can Do It pageant, and I have gone to Maryland a few times to visit her.

You know how people always say they just need one person who understands them? I had never really had that one person and, well, now I was surrounded by literally dozens of them. A lot of them had been told—as I was—that they were crazy for chasing after such big dreams. But when I got to Miss USA, I thought, *Now who's crazy? We made it!* Sometimes it felt like I must be dreaming, but it was real.

Miss USA is when my life changed forever. I am a different person for having had that experience. Miss USA is a true sisterhood, and although we don't see one another every day and we don't get an opportunity to chat that often, the moment one of us needs anything, we are there for one another, and I am so blessed to have that in my life.

Even today, when I am struggling with something, I can just send an email to any of the other girls, and they immediately understand how I feel and can help me figure out what I should say and do. I feel bad that every woman in the world doesn't have the same privilege.

One of the many things that make my Miss USA sisters so cool is that they are able to admit their mistakes and talk about them and, because of it, become stronger and better people. I didn't realize it until then, but when you're insecure, it's hard to handle the fact that you make mistakes. But the Miss USA girls were confident enough to face their flaws and try to improve them. Because of that, Miss USA was not only the most exciting thing I had ever done, it was the most comforting, too. In a way, those weeks were an otherworldly experience. I could hardly believe it was happening to me. And when I look back at it now, it's as if I was floating on clouds, gazing down from someplace high in the sky at my body below. I mean, I just had to keep reminding myself to breathe, reminding my heart to beat, because it was as if I had died and gone to heaven.

FOURTEEN
Winning Isn't Everything

efore I arrived in Las Vegas, the pageant organizers had offered to hire a professional escort for me. But I was looking to prove I could do anything the other girls could do; I wanted to show that I was good enough and could measure up to them. So I said, "Thank you, but I won't need an escort at all until pageant night."

After the first day of hours and hours of walking, I gave in. I didn't want to, but having help for this one problem makes my life so much easier, and as much as I wished I could do without it, I was grateful for the assistance.

No one made me feel bad that I was the only girl who needed an escort. And, as the days went by, I began to realize that I really didn't need to prove myself to the organization or to the other contestants. I could see that they knew I was capable of doing whatever I set my mind to.

The fact that the organizers had gone to the trouble of hiring an escort for me—not only for the pageant but for every day of the three weeks I was there—I have to admit, it gave me a certain satisfaction to think about how wrong those nasty people on the message boards were when they claimed the pageant organizers wouldn't even let me compete.

My escort turned out to be the hottest man who ever walked the face of the earth; Rocky Fain was his name. Rocky is tall and dark, ripped and confident. He was a wonderful help to me and incredibly sweet. Rocky was a professional escort for the stars, who took him to parties and events so they wouldn't have to go alone. It's a shame they don't offer those services in my hometown, because having an escort would have saved me a lot of embarrassment and heartache, whether it was going down the hall at school or walking into that one party the cool kids invited me to. He had been an escort for Paris Hilton and Britney Spears . . . and now he was helping me?!?! I could hardly believe it!

In a lot of ways, Rocky was like Keith: He was a funny guy who wanted to make me feel good. He knew I was ashamed that I needed to hold on to him, but he never made me feel uncomfortable about it—and he always did everything he possibly could to reassure me. He would smile and take my arm gently, and tell me I looked pretty. And then he'd say, "Don't worry, Abbey, we have this."

All the girls had to do a few dance routines and because I had to hold on to Rocky, he had to be in them. Since none of the other girls needed escorts, he was the only guy there. But I don't think he minded. In addition to the dance number, we also had the evening gown portion of the competition, which required walking down a very wide and long staircase with lights that shone beneath it. Going down that staircase in a floor-length gown and five-inch heels was a pretty terrifying experience, even with Rocky holding my hand. I mean, for one thing, the stairs are steep, and you have to look straight ahead and can never look down. And all the while, you have to keep smiling and acting as if it's perfectly normal to mosey down a giant staircase all dressed up while a couple thousand people are sitting there watching. But Rocky promised that we would be fine. And I trusted him. In practices, I came very close to falling a few times, and each time he steadied me so quickly that no one even noticed.

We rehearsed the staircase walk and the dance number

in our high heels. After hours of that, my feet started giving out. I couldn't bear to put weight on them. But once again, Rocky reassured me that it wouldn't be a problem. He said I could hold on to him and put about half my weight on him as long as I made sure my hand looked loose on his arm and didn't look as if I was desperately gripping him. So even though that's exactly what I was doing, there was no way you could tell. Rocky made it look easy and natural. He was always saying, "Don't be a chicken, you can do this." And on pageant night he gave me a stuffed animal: a big chicken that dances and sings. Can you imagine anyone so adorable? And did I mention he smelled amazing?

I will never forget the moment when we finally went into the ballroom where the pageant was held and I got to see the stage for the very first time—the same stage I had seen on TV for years. *The* Miss USA stage! And here I was on it. I couldn't help it: I cried. I thought, *How did I get to compete in the Miss USA pageant!?!?! How in the world do you go from a hog farm to being Miss Iowa!?*

As the pageant drew nearer, we went to so many incredible places in Las Vegas. Some were so cool and expensive that I'll probably never be able to go to them again. One night we went to an event at a very high-class Italian restaurant. Well, buttered noodles are my absolute favorite dish, and on this night we were served big bowls of yummy ravioli. I didn't even ask what was in it but when I started eating it I realized it was the most delish pasta I had ever had. It melted in my mouth. After a few giant bites, I realized that the stuffing in the ravioli was light gray and very soft. I noticed some of the girls weren't eating it and finally I asked why. There was a good reason: The meat was veal. Now, you'd think a farm girl like me wouldn't get too upset by this, but it made me supernauseated to think I'd just inhaled a baby cow. The other thing about farm girls is that we get to know the animals—we pet them, we feed them, we give them names. That aspect of life on the farm is a big part of me. So all I could think about was a tiny baby cow just trying to walk—and I had eaten him. I decided from then on that I would slow down when I get to a fancy restaurant and make sure to find out what I'm being served before I eat it!

The Miss USA Organization had a big room for us on the same floor of the hotel where we were staying. This big room was filled with refrigerators stocked with bottles of water, juice, yogurt, and fruit, and occasionally, they put out cookie platters. By the time we'd arrive back at the hotel after rehearsals, my feet were blistered and I was too tired to walk there, even though it wasn't far. Instead, my roommate would go and bring back chocolate chip cookies. Vincenza had more willpower than I did, and she'd eat just one and leave three or four others on our nightstand. Well, I'd be lying in bed, feeling hungry after dinner. Those cookies were so tempting, finally I would give in and eat every last one. She'd laugh and watch me eat and say she was living vicariously through me. I have no regrets about eating those cookies. For one thing, they were really good. For another, they gave me the energy to put my heels back on my aching and blistered feet the next day and do it with a big smile on my face and a big fat delicious cookie in my mouth.

By the time the pageant actually began, I had soaked up every single second of our three-week stay. Each day had seemed more perfect than the ones before it, and I didn't want the experience to end. Having come to Las Vegas feeling that I didn't belong, I finally felt like that I did belong with these women, who I admired not just for their beauty, but for their hearts. It was as if someone had lifted a weight off my shoulders—I felt free to say whatever I wanted, and to say it without any fear that the others would look at me like I was nuts and judge me.

But of course, nothing is totally perfect, and there's one night that I'll always regret. It was a red-carpet event on the Vegas strip to introduce all the contestants. There were lots of people and cameras and film crews and we were all supposed to introduce ourselves in some kind of original way. Well, I was representing Iowa: I couldn't say "I'm from the state where you can click your heels together and always find your way home" or "I'm from the state with the big apple." So what did I do? I made my pig noise, which actually does sound just like a pig. OMG! The people from the media were staring at me like I must have lost my mind! I guess I could have said something really simple like: "I'm Abbey Curran, a hog farmer's daughter from the great state of Iowa." That wouldn't have been very exciting, that's for sure, but at least I would have come across as a normal human being!

FIFTEEN
An Amazing Night

The pageant was held in the theater of the Planet Hollywood Resort and Casino. On the opening night, the stage for Miss USA looked absolutely magical. Everything sparkled: the staircase and floor, the thousands of Swarovski crystals in the giant chandeliers decorating the stage, and the twinkling light created by all of the sequins and crystals on our gowns as reflected in the brilliant lights.

That night, I was more nervous than I have ever been in my life. Backstage, I stood beside Rocky while each of the girls was introduced in pretaped segments projected onto three giant video screens. There was Miss Alabama . . . Miss California . . . Miss Georgia . . . Finally, I heard the announcer say, "Miss Iowa USA! Abbey Curran!"

Then I appeared on the screens, seated in a quaint little boat like the ones they have in Venice, Italy, which was being rowed by a gondolier standing in the back of it. I looked up and said, "Abbey Curran, Miss Iowa USA."

People clapped and cheered. My parents and my grandparents were there, along with my friend Tessa and the physical therapist I'd had when I was a child. Listening to that cheering from backstage gave me the most overwhelming feeling, and even as I smiled, I had tears spilling from my eyes. After that, a Rihanna song came on over the loudspeakers. It was time for all of us to make our entrance onto the stage for the opening dance number. I was shaking. I was about to step onto the same stage I had seen on TV for years. I was actually competing in the Miss USA pageant; me, who so many people had seen as this pitiful crippled girl who came to school in a truck that smelled of hog manure and had to hold on to her daddy's hand.

As all fifty-one girls came onstage to dance, chills were running through my veins. My heart was beating so fast I could hardly take a breath. Being on the Miss USA stage was an experience that I knew was given to me as a gift from God.

After we danced, we changed into our evening gowns and came back onto the stage, into the spotlight, one by one. This was the night the judges would determine which girls were in the top ten, though the names would not be announced until the following evening when the pageant was televised.

I grasped Rocky's hand as we stepped onto the staircase. I smiled the biggest smile ever as we made our way down the stairs, and it was all I could do not to cry tears of joy again.

I'll never forget it. It was more beautiful and wonderful than anything I'd experienced in my entire life.

The second night of the pageant is shown on live TV. The lights on the stage felt very bright as we all came out and performed the dance number. After that, they announced who was in the top ten. I was among the forty-one girls who didn't make it, but honestly, I didn't mind. Just being there was the top of everything for me. After we were "eliminated," we had to change into our swimsuits anyway, since everyone who isn't in the top ten has to hurry back onstage and dance in the background while the girls in the top ten changed into swimsuits for the final judging.

While we danced, Lou was backstage screaming at all forty-one of us, "You are sexy!!!! You are beautiful! And you are the hottest ladies in the country!"

Then we walked off just in time for the first of the top ten girls to appear.

As thrilled as I was to be in the pageant, I was also relieved that the pressure was off after three weeks of being in Las Vegas and appearing at events and rehearsing and giving interviews and going to dinners where we said, "No, thank you" to anything delicious. I wasn't the only one who felt that way. As we were changing into swimsuits, Miss Ohio said, "Where are those chocolate chip cookies? Let's eat them all. It doesn't matter now!"

After the pageant I was flown out to Los Angeles to be on *The Ellen DeGeneres Show*. I was really surprised she wanted me on it. It was pretty scary. For one thing, I had no idea what to wear. I really stink, stylewise. So I wore a pair of black dress pants that ended at the knee, black heels, and a royal blue, super-tight-fitting shirt that was too short, so the pageant chaperone traveling with me tied a black satin ribbon around my waist. I was backstage when someone came over to me and said, "Ellen will come and get you."

That made me really nervous, because I was concerned that she wouldn't know how to walk with me. But she did. She made it easy. I just wish a different song had played when I walked out. It was Christina Aguilera's song "Beautiful," which has this lyric: "I am beautiful no matter what they say. Words can't bring me down." To be really honest, it made me feel pathetic. I would have preferred "Isn't She Lovely," but I always get the sad songs, the broken-wing songs. Still, I know that someday people will be aware of all the things that challenged people can do, and this will change.

Actually, there were other songs that reminded me of what an unbelievable experience the Miss USA pageant had been. For months afterward—well, to tell you the truth, for years after—I would play "Shut Up and Drive," the Rihanna song we competed to during the pageant. From the first second I hear it, it gives me that body-chilling, heart-stopping feeling. It takes me right back to standing on that stage.

People ask me, "You've heard that song a hundred times, why do you keep playing it?" But I couldn't help it then and I still play it now, because I can never be reminded too much of the very best feelings I ever had.

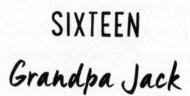

SIXTEEN
Grandpa Jack

When I came back home after the Miss USA pageant, I had to face some tough realities about my grandpa Jack. He was so proud that I was in the pageant and this meant the world to me, since he had been the first person to ever believe I could compete in an event of that sort. But even then it was clear that his age was starting to show and that he was slipping into dementia, which is a terrible condition that affects the brain. Because of dementia, he got many things confused. For instance, he was convinced that I had won Miss USA and he would tell everyone he saw that I had. Frankly, the fact that he got that one wrong didn't make me all that sad.

There were other things, though. At home he refused to take off his cowboy boots, and he kept tripping over the thick braided rugs my grandmother made. Everyone trips on those rugs, including me, but if Grandma took them away, then it was a sure thing that he'd have slipped on the polished floor.

My grandma was having a really hard time handling my grandfather, and eventually she and my mother arranged for him to be moved to an assisted-living home. It was a nice place, but he hated it. He missed his own furniture, so Grandma had the living room couch and his favorite chair and his desk moved there, but he still hated it, and that upset her so much she finally moved him back home. She always made sure that he could get where he wanted to go, whether it was to a particular restaurant or an auction at the Sale Barn. He insisted on going to the Hog Days Parade, but he couldn't sit with the hot sun beating down on him in the grandstand, so Grandma brought his lawn chair and set it up for him in the shade.

When I was away at college, I would talk to him on the phone, and a lot of times he would still seem pretty much okay. But he got worse and worse, and then his health began to fail. He went downhill pretty quickly. When I went to visit him in the weeks before he died, he was on oxygen and could no longer talk, and it was the most upsetting thing I'd ever seen.

He wasn't eating or drinking, and Grandma would swab his mouth. I would sit and hold his hand. When I talked to him he would open his eyes. He always knew it was me and that made me feel good. And then he was gone.

The day he died was a heartbreaking day.

At the funeral, I gave his eulogy. I wanted what I said to sound like him, so I talked the way he used to talk, which meant I said a cuss word here and there, and everyone was scandalized. I didn't know you can't say those things in a Catholic church!

I was asked by my grandma Wink to be one of his pallbearers, and that was a really big deal to me, partly because you're supposed to have men or boys do it, and also because people would assume, "Abbey's disabled, she can't help carry a casket." But they all knew that Grandpa Jack loved me so much and would have wanted me to be one of the people given the honor of carrying him out.

Losing Grandpa Jack was the most awful thing that had happened to me. I could hardly wrap my mind around it. The reality of it didn't kick in right away. But eventually it did, and all I can say now is that I believe Grandpa Jack is looking down at me all the time. He is my guardian angel now, and always, and forever.

SEVENTEEN
HBO

In the weeks before I went to the Miss USA pageant, I had gotten a call from a woman who said she was from *People* magazine. She said they wanted to do an article about me, and my first thought was that it had to be a hoax. But when I got a second phone call from her and was told they wanted to put me in their "Heroes Among Us" column, I realized it was true, and I was in awe.

I had been in my dorm room at school with my roommate Sarah when that second call came in. Usually, I wouldn't share that kind of news because I don't want people to be my friend only because something like that happens to me. I want real friends—I think everyone does. But Sarah had proven that she was a real friend, and she already knew everything about me, so I told her, and she was really excited about it. Actually, I think it was easier for her to believe than it was for me.

That night, we got dressed up and went to a fancy Italian restaurant to celebrate. It was in Davenport, and we ordered stuff I didn't know about before, like bruschetta. It was an occasion to be like the awesome people we wanted to pretend we were.

The plan for the article in *People* was that I would pose for a picture first, and then I'd be interviewed when I got to the Miss USA pageant. So on the day of the photo shoot, I headed off to Cedar Rapids, Iowa, which is about a two-hour drive from my college. The shoot was going to be done in a studio, and there was a small team there when I arrived: a photographer and his assistant sent there by the magazine from New York City, a hairstylist and makeup artist. I was so excited. Everyone was so nice; it was wonderful.

The photographers were very professional and detail-oriented and went right to work getting things set up while I went into hair and makeup. I have to admit that, contrary to what people assume about pageant girls, having my hair and makeup done is not my absolute favorite thing; I've always had a love/hate relationship with it. At first, I love sitting in the chair and having people apply the makeup and play with my hair. But when it's all said and done, even though I loved the pampering, I always end up with the sneaking suspicion that I could have done it better myself. Or maybe it's the fact that it never looks like "me" when they are finished. Luckily in this case, the hairstylist and makeup artist turned out to be a fantastic woman whose name is Andrea. She told me about all of the TV shows she had worked on and all the stars she had worked with, and I thought, *Well, if she can do them, then she is way overqualified for me.* I mean, it really was hard to believe. How could it be that a reporter from *People* magazine would want to come all the way out to some small town in Iowa to do a story on *me*, who had driven those two hours to the studio with a box of McDonald's chicken nuggets in my lap and hot rollers in my hair? I just had to go with the idea that I was meant to be there. I told myself, *Everything happens for a reason!*

For the first pictures the photographer took, they wanted me to be wearing my bikini. I think they expected me to be shy about that, but I had worked so hard to get into shape, and on top of that, I knew how surprising it would be to most people that a "disabled" girl had a superfit body—and I got to show it off.

After the bikini, the photographer wanted me to pose in my stunning peacock blue evening gown. I didn't think the photo did the dress justice, even though that's the photo that was used in the article. But I can't complain. The big thing was that *People* wanted my picture in their magazine!

I had been interviewed for the article while I was in Las Vegas, and so was Vincenza, my roommate. I had had no idea what she'd told them, so I was happy to read what she'd said about me: "She has a great personality. . . . She is so determined. Nothing can stop her." I thought that was really nice. The reporter had asked me a bunch of questions. I liked that one of the quotes she picked is what I answered when she asked if I worried about winning or about how I would look onstage. I had told her, "I'd love to win, but honestly, I'm so happy I got to be here. I believe it's the heart that matters the most, then I'll worry about the hair."

The article had come out about a week before the pageant ceremony and judging. I was thrilled. And that article ended up making a huge difference in my life, because it grabbed the attention of a documentary filmmaker named Ron Davis.

Soon after the article was published, Ron called me and said he wanted to film the Miss You Can Do It pageant. My first reaction was that it was weird that he was interested in my pageant, especially because he told me that he had just finished filming a drag queen pageant and I didn't see how one person could be interested in two such different things. Beyond that, the idea of someone filming my precious girls made me nervous, but I said I would think about it. By this time, Miss You Can Do It was heading into its sixth year, and I had established a board of directors who helped organize and oversee each pageant. So I asked them what they thought, and they were hesitant, too.

Keep in mind that Miss You Can Do It is my baby. It came from my dreams brought to reality: dreams to be of help and to make the world a better place. When I won the Miss Iowa pageant and when I competed for Miss USA, it was Miss You Can Do It that inspired me, and it was the girls who compete in that pageant who gave me a reason far greater than myself to go out there and try to crack that heavy glass ceiling that keeps us down. Everything I do in life I do for "my girls" who take part, or will take part someday, in Miss You Can Do It. Without those girls, I wouldn't be who I am now.

Was I going to let this random stranger who saw me in a *People* magazine article come in and film my sweet, beautiful girls? He told me to watch his documentary *Pageant*, which featured the 2005 Miss Gay America female impersonator and followed five drag queens as they competed in the pageant. The documentary had won a lot of awards, but to me, it was kind of a large jump from drag queens to girls with challenges. So I didn't watch the film at first. Then I figured, you never know unless you try, and I finally watched it—and it was really good. Ron made you understand drag queens; he took a subject that had the possibility of being a turnoff and made it understandable and even made you admire people you hadn't admired before. So I went to my pageant board again and we decided to allow Ron Davis to come and film us.

Ron is a handsome guy with huge, bright-blue eyes. He's very talkative and gestures a lot with his hands. He's dressed to the nines and he's gay and makes no bones about it. He's also funny and sweet and knew how to use his charm to get me to agree to whatever he wanted. For instance, he wanted to film me without any makeup on and let the cameras roll while I was getting pulled together, from start to finish. Yikes! For America to see it? I never left the house without makeup, and I was sure I'd scare away every man who might ever have interest in me. Still, I did it because he convinced me to do it. I kept hoping he wouldn't put it in the finished film, but he did.

He and his crew came twice to film the Miss You Can Do It pageants, first in 2008 and then a year later. He was going to show this film to the people in the HBO documentary department and if they gave him the go-ahead, the plan was for him to come back to Kewanee and film the pageants in 2010 and 2011. Having a film crew there got everyone excited, although their presence made for certain problems. They were very visible throughout the events and insisted on stopping the pageant at some key moments so they could film something again or film it from a different angle. I would say, "Bring in the contestants!" and they would tell me, "Wait, wait, wait, we didn't get that. Do it again." Or they'd say that they needed me to step back or move up, or go to the side, or stand under a particular light, or whatever. So a pageant that should have lasted two hours took forever and became the longest pageant in the history of the world, starting at five in the afternoon and ending at midnight. The poor little contestants were falling asleep.

Ron filmed the two pageants, and when he finished, he went back to New York City to put the documentary together. He talked about taking it to the Sundance Film Festival, which is a superfamous event that happens every winter in Utah. But I am such a rube that I wrote it down in my diary as the Sun Dance Film Festival—I had no clue about what it was. But anyway, it sounded good, though I really didn't expect to ever see Ron again.

Even if the documentary never happened, the pageant was becoming more and more known. And for that reason, not long after Ron had stopped filming, I was named the Most Inspirational Woman in America at the Inspiration Awards that benefit the great Susan G. Komen Foundation, which does so much for breast cancer awareness.

You can imagine how stunned and grateful and happy I was, and not just for myself, but because of what it could possibly mean for the pageant. The award was given in Los Angeles, and some of that year's winners in other categories were the anchorwoman Diane Sawyer and the pioneering anthropologist Dr. Jane Goodall. I was also awarded the Next Generation Award, which is given to someone they consider to be a leader of the future. Imagine that! Christina Applegate was there too and also won an award; another person at the awards was Lisa Vanderpump from *The Real Housewives of Beverly Hills*. I had no idea who either of them were, but luckily my mother had come with me to the awards and she watches E! and Bravo, and she told me. We had a great time. I still can hardly believe I was in a room with so many amazing women.

* * *

As the months went by and I didn't hear from Ron, I assumed nothing would happen. I mean, why would it? Why would anyone at HBO be interested in a documentary about challenged girls at a pageant in a tiny town they'd never heard of?

Nearly a year passed, and I had all but forgotten about the documentary. I wasn't disappointed because I never really thought anything would happen. Then Ron called me and said there were some people at HBO who actually *were* interested in it. Honestly, I didn't take that too seriously, either. A few months later, Ron called again and said that Sheila Nevins, the president of HBO Documentary Films, wanted to meet me.

What?!?!? Pinch me, someone! I must be dreaming!

After years of pleading with local vendors and begging my dad for money, and crying and praying and begging some more, was it really possible that this little pageant was actually about to be put on the map? Ron said that he needed me to come to New York City for the meeting with Sheila. I had never been there, but I had imagined what it must be like. From what I'd seen on TV and in the movies, I pictured beautiful women strolling along Fifth Avenue in gorgeous clothes, nannies in crisp uniforms wheeling babies in Central Park, and handsome men going to work on Madison Avenue. My mother had never been to New York City, either, and she wanted to come with me—I'm her only kid and she never wants to miss out.

So a few weeks later, there we were, checking into the Millennium Broadway Hotel in Times Square, which is this huge, wide, amazing street packed with theaters and thousands and thousands of colored lights and dozens of taxicabs and giant signs advertising all kinds of things and hundreds of people hurrying along and street vendors all over the place selling hot dogs and roasted chestnuts. Our room looked out over the city where skyscrapers were gleaming in the late-afternoon light. I couldn't believe how lucky I was to be there, and having my mother there with me was so special. She was the one who always insisted that I could never quit on commitments I'd made, no matter what. She was also one of my role models because she was a nurse who had dedicated herself to helping others. I shared that dedication, and because of it, the Miss You Can Do It pageant was flourishing, and my mother and I were in New York City, gazing down at the streets below, both of our heads full of dreams.

EIGHTEEN
Exactly What I Was Hoping For

I met Ron for breakfast the next morning and then we headed off to meet Sheila Nevins. For the big meeting, I had ordered a dress online from Victoria's Secret. As always, I thought I had packed the right outfit, until the day came when I had to wear it. It was a royal-blue dress and it was very short and very tight; I'd also brought clear Lucite heels. The shoes were the biggest mistake, because they were open-toed and it was snowing. This was an outfit that could have been great if I was competing for Miss USA. In fact, it's too bad I didn't own it when I went to Las Vegas. By the time we got to Sheila's apartment, I was superworried, as usual, about how I looked and what I would say. And knowing that the president of HBO Documentary Films was behind the door that was about to open made me so nervous that I could barely breathe. Keep in mind that I'm the person who got invited to exactly one high school party, and this meeting was a million times bigger and more important than any party I might have gone to before.

But then the door opened and we entered the coolest, most stylish apartment I had ever been in, where we were greeted by a beautiful woman in black pants and a white sweater. That was her—Sheila Nevins. My first thought was that I had never seen anyone who was more amazing. She is this incredibly powerful woman, but she's kind and beautiful and was nice to me and wanted my dreams to come true. Holy smokes!!! That's new!!! She was put together well but not superdressed up, and had flawless skin, the perfect shade of pink lipstick, tons of sparkly jewelry on, and her nails were done and her blond hair was perfect. Best of all, I soon found out that her heart was huge and that she and I were on the same page.

Before I got there, I thought meeting her would be sort of like a movie, where we'd be sipping sparkling water or champagne and eating caviar and saying "oh darling" this or that. But thank goodness it wasn't like that at all! The surroundings were elegant, but at the same time everything was very relaxed, and being with

Sheila was an unbelievable experience. I hope I can have her inner beauty one day. When I say I want to be a powerful woman, what I mean is that I want to be like Sheila.

She explained that she had seen me and the Miss You Can Do It pageant in the documentary footage Ron had shot and submitted to film festivals. She said she had been so impressed by me and what I was doing. I think my eyes must have been the size of dinner plates as she told me all of this. I could hardly believe that this amazing woman was impressed with me! I couldn't believe she had actually wanted to meet me and had paid to bring me to New York City to meet her!

When Sheila and Ron and I talked about making the documentary, all sorts of different ideas would come up, and each time, Sheila would turn to me and she'd say, "What do you think, Abbey?"

It was exactly what I was hoping for.

I learned a lot from watching Sheila. She isn't afraid to tell someone they are in the wrong, and she isn't afraid to speak her mind, but she does it with graciousness and class. If she had competed in Miss USA, she would have won because she is so confident and educated and stands out in a crowd. Even if you didn't know who she was, you would assume she was important—she just looks the part.

To have someone so powerful be so kind and believe in me . . . well, I can never find the words to thank her for that. I told her my dreams about creating a perfect hospital, and reporting on stories about bullying, and expanding the Miss You Can Do It pageant, and she didn't laugh or roll her eyes. Instead, she said, "Yes. I think those things will happen." She laughed, smiled, ate a sandwich, spilled a bit of it on her sweater, and was still beautiful. Actually, that made her even more beautiful.

Sheila's belief in me made a big difference in the way I saw myself. It helped me to see that I wasn't a caterpillar anymore and gave me hope that I might become a full-fledged butterfly!

Just being around Sheila Nevins made me feel good, and when she said we were friends and gave me her phone number, I couldn't believe it. It melted my heart. This totally cool, gorgeous woman, inviting me to be her friend???!!!!! Phone the press!!! Never saw that coming!

At one point, I told her I loved her earrings; she pulled them off and gave them to me. When she noticed my open-toed heels, she sent her assistant out to get me a pair of Ugg boots. They felt so soft and warm and snug-gly. I couldn't get over how thoughtful it was of her to get me the best boots ever. She also gave me a pair of great seats and backstage passes for me and my mother to the Broadway show *Chicago*. Later, she sent me gor-geous gifts. She even picked out my incredible little shih tzu when I decided to get a dog. I couldn't decide which puppy to pick, so I sent her some pictures and she chose. And she must have chosen right, because I have the best little dog!

I want to be as powerful as Sheila so I can do for other people what she did for me.

A few months after visiting New York, I went on a trip with Ron and his producer Julie Anderson to look for girls who would be in the pageant and the documentary. We needed to find girls whose families were willing to be interviewed and filmed at home. I agreed with Ron's idea of using home footage to introduce the audience to the girls and their parents before they saw them at the pageant. I felt it was important to show the struggle involved in their everyday lives and how, even in the worst situations possible, these families and girls make it through and don't become mean or bitter. They learn to look on the bright side. People who have challenges usually remember that whatever they're facing, it's worth being grateful because it could always be worse.

In one case, we filmed a small-town family, a dad and a mom, two sweet little sons, and two little girls who have Down syndrome. The documentary shows how someone spray-painted horrible language all over their house and their car. But instead of becoming hateful, this family moved forward, and they taught their children to learn from their example. In another instance, we filmed a happy, adorable little girl showing you around her house, moving through it in her wheelchair. She showed it off so proudly you might think she was living in a beautiful place in Beverly Hills, but her house is actually in the middle of nowhere and it's a trailer.

Julie, Ron, and I traveled all over the Midwest together, interviewing and filming. Along the way, there were all sorts of problems with scheduling, and sometimes we'd get to a location where we needed to shoot outdoors and then rain poured down for the next few days. Julie was always there to smooth things over and make whatever adjustments were necessary. Along the way, they taught me about the wonders of sushi, though their chopstick lessons were unsuccessful. This country girl just stabs the pieces of raw fish with her fork.

The days were long, and sometimes the shoots

became frustrating, especially when Ron wanted me to walk everywhere we went so he could film me walking. I HATE having people see me walk, and having a camera crew follow my every awkward move was not fun! I would protest, but Ron would smile that charming smile of his and say I had to do it. So I did it, because in the end, anything I did for the documentary was something I was doing for my girls. Another thing I didn't like was having to spend the entire day with a microphone attached to me. Do you know how embarrassing it is to be traveling for hours in a van of people you don't know who are hearing all of the sounds your stomach makes in the course of a day? But Ron would push for it, even after I said, "No, I'm sorry, but I can't." He never lost his smile—in fact, he'd smile bigger and say, "Okay, but we have to, so let's do it."

There were definitely moments when I wanted to kill him. But then I would remind myself that I was doing all this for my girls, who have even more challenges than I ever had. The fact is, I am so thankful to Ron now because without him I would never have had an HBO documentary, and who knows where Miss You Can Do It would be without that? Plus, it was such a fun spring, and Julie, Ron, and I really bonded. I don't think I'll ever forget them and what they have done for me.

216

Our tour to film girls and their families ended in June, and the pageant was in August. A few days before it began, Ron and Julie and their crew pulled into Kewanee in their rented SUVs. Everyone in town knew they were from HBO and knew they were there because of me. A lot of people, especially ones I knew from high school, were amazed by this. Of course they wouldn't have been surprised if the crew and their cameras were there because of Rachel . . . but for Abbey Curran? That's something no one would have anticipated, and it made having HBO there even sweeter.

Ron interviewed me for the documentary in my high school, at my old locker, in the hallway where I'd gotten laughed at and where I'd fallen down. Now, I was miked up and made up and being filmed by several cameras. I could never have imagined it happening in my wildest dreams. I kept thinking of all the times someone had said to me, "Oh, Abbey, you can't do that!" Well . . . remember what I told you: When people say I can't do something, I say, "Watch me." And now the people in my town, people I'd known my whole life, were really watching. I have to think they were more than a little stunned because they could see that, in spite of everything, I was making something of my life and—better than that—making a difference in the lives of others.

My birthday was on the pageant weekend that year. Normally my birthday is pretty uneventful, but this year I was given a surprise birthday party by the entire HBO crew. They got me a big, beautiful white buttercream birthday cake with raspberry filling, not to mention the greatest gifts. They had really done their homework, because I love Victoria's Secret, and they had gotten me an unbelievably generous Victoria's Secret gift card. Then there was a perfectly wrapped box with paper in different shades of blue, my favorite color, and a giant blue bow on the top. I knew it had to be from the wonderful Sheila Nevins—and it was. Inside were the most beautiful giant crystal dangle earrings and crystal bracelets and rings—and luckily, no necklaces. If you knew me well you'd know that I don't wear necklaces because with the way I walk, necklaces swing side to side and whack me in the face, and the last thing I need is to bring more attention to my situation. The jewelry was beautiful, and it was very special that someone so important all the way in New York City remembered my birthday. Those things mean a lot, and I don't forget them. It was a great party and the whole time I was thinking, *This is something Kim Kardashian would get . . . not me.*

The pageant took place a few days later, and when the shoot ended, Ron said he was happy with how it all went, but I had no idea if he was just saying that to make me feel better or if he really meant it. I sure hoped he meant it, because by then I could see what a benefit the documentary would be to my girls.

NINETEEN
Another Trip to New York City

A few months later my mother and I were on another plane to New York City, where we were going to see the finished documentary. Sheila Nevins took us to lunch and afterward she said she had a surprise for me. All three of us got into a waiting car and the driver took us to a huge store in Koreatown, where there are city blocks filled with shops that sell the most gorgeous costume jewelry. We went into one store where there must have been thousands and thousands of items, packed wall to wall. And I really mean walls of it! Huge walls! There were rhinestones, crystals, AB crystals, Swarovski crystals, studs and hoops and dangle earrings and full chandelier earrings. At one point my mother had to tell me to close my mouth because everyone could see that I was drooling!

Sheila said, "Get what you want." I was in heaven! But how could I choose? I was overwhelmed, so Sheila handed me a little plastic basket and we went down the rows together, and as we walked, she took my arm and let me hold on to her. She'd ask, "Abbey, do you like this?" And if I said yes, she'd throw it in the basket; if I said I loved it, she would throw in two or three of the same piece, "just in case one breaks." She led me down many, many rows, and if I was looking at two things and couldn't decide, she'd put both of them in the basket. It was so amazing; I couldn't stop smiling.

But I never feel comfortable having people buy me things, unless it's someone in my immediate family, like my dad or my grandpa Jack. So I had my own money in my hand ready to go, but Sheila held on to the basket of stuff and bought it all. That day I got more jewelry and sparkly things than I will ever know what to do with. Whenever you see me wearing any type of bling, you can thank Sheila Nevins for it.

Looking back, I wish I had videotaped that afternoon, because it was a once-in-a-lifetime thing, like the Miss USA pageant. Imagine: the president of HBO Documentary Films being kind enough to stop her busy life and take the farm girl down to crowded Koreatown. Honestly, I can't wait to go back to New York City. It's such an exciting place, and I think it's where dreams can really come true.

It was late afternoon when we headed back to HBO for the private showing of the documentary, which had been titled *Miss You Can Do It*. I put on some of the superpretty jewelry and a little lipstick before we met with the rest of the HBO documentary department, who were also going to watch the film. Being in a theater at the HBO headquarters made me feel as if I was part of entertainment history. I could only imagine the people who had walked through that door and sat in these seats before me. There were only a few people there that day, including Julie and Ron and some HBO executives and my mother, Sheila, and me.

As the lights dimmed, Sheila and Ron and Julie and my mom all looked at me and smiled. I felt like they wanted me to say something, but I was so nervous that for once in my life I had nothing to say. I had no idea what Ron had put in the documentary. All I could think was, *I hope they like it.*

It was an honor to watch the documentary with them. At the same time, it was awkward because I couldn't help being emotional. The documentary begins with me winning Miss Iowa, the day my dream came true. It was such an unexpected surreal moment then and still is for me, and when I saw it on HBO's big screen, I cried, just like I did when I won. Everyone kept looking down the row at me to see my reactions, so I tried to hold back my tears. I don't like to cry in public, even if it's the happy kind of crying.

As we watched, I was paying attention to the rest of the audience. I felt so good every time I heard their *ooh*s and *aah*s. I loved watching the pageant on the big screen. That was amazing! I don't necessarily like seeing myself because all I can think of is what I would have said or done differently. But I was so proud of my girls and their families, who came across beautifully. You could see the girls' bravery and determination as they coped with daily difficulty and pain. And that made it all the more special when they took part in the Miss You Can Do It pageant, to see the joy on their beautiful, beaming faces. The documentary ended with me walking down the hallway of my school, with that herky-jerky walk I never want anyone to see. Then the lights came on and everyone clapped, and that was pretty cool! The HBO people said they were thrilled with it. And I loved it! It was better than I could have dreamed.

A year or so later, my mother, my grandma Wink, my dad, and I flew back to New York City and watched the documentary again at a premiere party that HBO hosted.

There were a lot of people in the audience, including some of the Miss You Can Do It girls who were in the documentary. I thought it was so great of HBO to bring them to New York City to see it. It was so important to me that they liked what they saw—and they did. After the screening ended I had to do a question-and-answer session hosted by a distinguished journalist named John Hockenberry. He is someone who has worked in TV and radio and won three Peabody Awards. He's also a disability rights activist and he's disabled himself, having been in a terrible car accident that wasn't his fault. It happened nearly forty years ago, when he was nineteen, and he has been confined to a wheelchair ever since. He was very nice to me, but—WOW!—New Yorkers are tough! The questions I got were not easy to answer. For instance, people in the audience asked how I feel about gays and would they be allowed in the pageant, and why don't I allow boys to enter. I had to be honest, of course, so I said the pageant is called MISS You Can Do It and my passion is to run a beauty pageant for women. That's what I have experience with. I have no problem with someone starting a similar pageant for men, but it's not my area of expertise. What made me even more nervous than I might have been was that Sheila Nevins was in the audience *and* Rachel! Yes, THE Rachel, the beautiful track star and high school class president who was so cool she could afford to be my friend; Rachel, the person I had always measured myself against. She had taken a train from New Jersey, where she was working as an engineer. She had heard about the documentary through Facebook, and she got in touch with me. I mentioned that the premiere was in New York City, and she showed up and sat right by me. Having Rachel there made it a superspecial night.

After the questions and answers, we all moved down the hall to a beautiful room where everything was decorated in shades of pink. There were free drinks and mini grilled cheese sandwiches and shrimp cocktail . . . my favorite!

While I was standing with Rachel, a man came up to me and introduced himself. He was an executive at HBO and he told me that the company was going to donate $10,000 to the Miss You Can Do It pageant. I about fell over and died right there, but being me I just cried like a baby and looked a mess. That was by far the biggest donation that we had ever received, and it would cover a large portion of the pageant for that year. It was a huge relief to not have to worry about raising money for a while—just when I thought I couldn't be any more grateful to HBO for making the documentary!

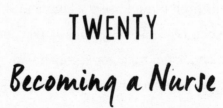

TWENTY
Becoming a Nurse

I come from a family of nurses: Both of my grand-mothers were nurses and my mom still is. Even when I was entering pageants and later, when I was thinking about what sort of career I wanted to have, I always recognized that caring for others was more important to me than anything else. Which is why I realized that if I didn't become a nurse like my mother and grandmothers, I would regret it for the rest of my life.

I am now twenty-six years old and enrolled in nursing school. I wish I could tell you I am getting straight As, that I have a wonderful fiancé, and that I am jet-setting to all sorts of parties in New York and Paris and London, but that would be a lie. I am actually sitting in my mother's house (where we moved when I was in sixth grade and where I still live). In my lap is my little shih tzu called

Nevins—named for Sheila Nevins. I'm stressing about a test I took this morning. Not to mention clinicals, which you do when you're a student nurse. It means taking care of one or two or sometimes more patients a day. You give physical assessments, give meds and shots, do wound/dressing changes, and start IVs. Clinicals begin early in the morning and can go on until late at night.

I've always believed that being a nurse is one of the best things a person can be. Recently, I had an experience that proved that nursing isn't just a job—it's more like a calling. I believe this experience was a gift from God and was His way of keeping me grounded and showing me the important things. It happened when I went to the gynecologist for my yearly appointment and received results that turned my world upside down.

The doctor I go to practices in the Chicago suburbs, a two-hour drive from my home. I don't go to doctors in Kewanee because when you live in a small town, nothing stays confidential for long, and even little things become big news that gets passed around.

It was a routine physical exam, and afterward I decided to go shopping, which is the only thing to do when you're surrounded by the best boutiques! I came home, and a few days later my test results were sent to me online through a confidential medical site that my doctor's office uses. My test results were in full medical terminology. There were a lot of numbers and I couldn't tell exactly what they all meant, but the bottom line seemed to be that there was a strong possibility that I am infertile. Well, you know how much I want to have babies. So I was stunned. And there were no explanations. No further instructions. Just those numbers that were cold and stark and terrifying.

I received this message on a Sunday at midnight. Good timing, huh? There was no way to reach my doctor. I stayed awake most of the night. It's hard to sleep when you are thinking that one of the things you want most in the world may not be possible. On Monday, I called my doctor's office at 7:30 a.m. trying to get ahold of her. She wasn't there, but I spoke with the nurse, who couldn't tell me anything. By evening, when I still hadn't heard from the doctor, I was getting more freaked out by the minute. Finally, I ended up getting a phone message from the doctor at 8:00 p.m. I missed the call because I never imagined a doctor would call me at night like that . . . I had given up after five o'clock. If I had known she was so awesome that she would call that late, I would have sat watching my phone and waited for the call.

I was going crazy, so I decided to go to my old reliable

spot, Soderstrom Skin Institute. Yes, it's a place for dermatology and plastic surgery, but to specialize in those things, their medical providers have to get through basic health care first. There is a physician's assistant who works there who I like a lot. Her name is Michelle Roth, and as a PA, she is someone who can act as a doctor, do minor surgeries, write prescriptions, and see her own patients.

I remembered her as sweet and personable, and I knew she was also a small-town farmer's daughter who had grown up only a town over from me, so it was easy to call her parents and ask them to have her call me. And she did! This PA who I have met only twice was kind enough to call me back at 9:00 p.m., from home, on a Monday night. I gave her all the information I had. She kept telling me, "You are going to be okay, you are," and that meant a lot. She stayed on the phone with me for a good hour, explaining what the test results meant. She wasn't getting paid, she had called right from her cell phone, and she showed me what it is to be a wonderful health-care provider. She gave me something to strive for.

She also told me she'd help me whenever I needed it and I could text or call anytime. I am not sure why she cared so much, but she is one of those special people I will spend a lifetime trying to repay. Now that I am in school, working toward my master's in nursing so I can be a nurse practitioner, I keep moments of that day with me. They remind me that everyone just wants someone who understands and cares, someone who can relate to them. They show me that a little compassion can change someone's worst day or week into a good one. As it turned out, when I reached my doctor she decided to have me tested again. The result is that I can have babies. I don't think I have ever, in my entire life, been so relieved.

I always understood that being a nurse is a tough profession, but I didn't completely understand why. Now I see why my mom was so stressed: because you fall in love with the patients. You want to be there for them and make sure they are getting the best care possible. You start praying for your patients, and I don't think anyone who's not a nurse can understand exactly how you feel. It breaks your heart when there isn't an easy way—or any way—to fix them.

As part of my clinicals, one of the patients I was assigned to take care of is an elderly lady who wasn't doing well at all. I remember walking into her hospital room for the first time. It was extremely early in the morning and I had been running all week on about three hours of sleep a night. The hospital was overheated and

I felt hot and nauseated and awful. It turned out that this patient wasn't mobile. She was wearing Depends. Well, it takes a great deal of mental strength to walk into the room of someone who needs you to give her a bath, change her diaper, and replace the dressing on an open wound that gives off an odor that stays in your nose the rest of the day. This was a far cry from what I had imagined doing as a family nurse practitioner with happy, mostly healthy patients who come to you for in-and-out appointments. But I sucked it up because I had to. What happened is that I took one look at her chart and related many of her issues to the issues my grandpa Jack once had. I saw that her husband never left her side and kept saying he loved her. I will never forget how her husband would sit on her bed, holding her hand and discreetly wiping away the tears that ran down his face. He showed me pictures of the beautiful woman she had been, and I came to see her not only as a patient but also as a mother, a grandmother, a wife, and a best friend. I realized that so many people loved her so much. And although the patient in the bed looked nothing like that beautiful woman in the pictures, I knew it was her . . . and I began to empathize with her. It was not her fault that she was sick. And if she were a part of my family or a friend, I would want her to have excellent care. Although

I can't walk the best, I can be a caregiver who is as good as it gets. I was happy to give her a bath and to change those Depends and make her squeaky clean. I learned about her and I talked to her just as I would a friend. Although she didn't speak, she would make sounds or gestures sometimes. I know she knew what I was saying. When the doctor came in and spoke to her husband about the outcome, it was that she couldn't stay in the hospital and she couldn't go home without surgery, and the surgery would probably kill her. The husband held her hand and begged the doctor for another week. That was when I needed to leave the room, so they wouldn't see me when I broke down in sobs. I wanted to say, "Here's my number, I would love to come to your home and take care of her." But even if I was a nurse practitioner instead of a student, it wouldn't be right to do that. I was assigned to this sweet woman only for a few days, and then I was moved to a different room and a different patient. But I went in and visited her each day I was in clinicals, making sure she was taken care of. One day I went to the room and she was gone. I don't know what happened and I hate it. I worry about her, I pray for her, and it gives me a lump in my throat when I think of her. You know, I can't recite textbook definitions word for word and I don't remember every medication and what it does and how it works—I often have to look them up—and I may occasionally sneak my favorite light-pink nail polish on and wear it on hospital days even though I'm not supposed to. But one thing I can absolutely promise is that I truly care about my patients.

When I applied for nursing school, I was SO excited about it. And I didn't just get in, I got early acceptance. HOLY SMOKES! That meant I was in the accelerated program. They believed in me, and I was determined not to let them down.

Being in school hasn't changed, even though it's nursing school this time. There are still the cool girls, and then there is me. When I say the smallest thing sometimes I see them look at each other like I'm crazy or stupid, but now—after everything that has happened to me—I know that I am not. And honestly, I think if anything is stupid, it's rolling your eyes while someone—meaning me—is talking.

I am not the best nurse yet, but I do like to think I am the most compassionate. Because of the experience I had with that one elderly lady, I now look at the patients and think: they are somebody's mom, somebody's grandma, somebody's best friend. I think, *What if that was my mom or best friend, how would I want them to be taken care of?* I always have the same answer: with lots of love, compassion, and understanding, and that's what I try to give to my patients each day.

When I graduate, I want to be a nurse practitioner. It's a really great job because they basically do many of the things that doctors do: write prescriptions, see patients, admit patients, perform minor surgeries, and even deliver babies.

I think it's important for someone in my family to be in the medical field. For one thing, I want to be able to take care of my family members when they need it. Everyone has problems that come up in life, and they want their medical well-being to be in the hands of someone they can trust. Nursing school is hard. You care so much about your patients and their families and then you are supposed to walk out the hospital door and leave your work at work. That's been the most difficult part for me. The patients I've taken care of have left an impact on my heart, and although I moan and groan at the prospect of getting to the hospital by 6:30 a.m. Monday through Friday to work in overheated isolation rooms, when Saturday and Sunday come along, I wake up thinking about them, wondering, *How are they doing? Are they okay? Did someone remember to help them order their breakfast, do their dressing change? Did they get the right meds?* It makes

234

me mad when I hear nurses talk about patients and say, "Oh my gosh, this one is crazy." Because when I got the news about my test results, I was going crazy, too, and these patients can't call on Michelle Roth to save their day. So I don't mind crazy. I understand it. CP has certainly taught me the importance of approaching people with a lack of judgment and always treating them with kindness. I never want to be too good for anybody or anything.

Having CP still sets me apart. One of my professors gave me a funny look when I was taking care of a patient. All I was doing was carrying away a tray that had a full cup of coffee and a bowl of cereal on it. Kitchen workers come up and collect the trays, but as students we are taught to keep our patients' rooms clean. I really didn't need to remove the tray, but the patient wanted me to. And as I was carrying it the professor said, "Do you really think you can do this?"

I said, "I don't know, but if I can't, are you going to kick me out of the program?"

She said, "I'm not sure. I've never had anything like this before."

A few years ago, I wouldn't have known what to do, but now that I am older and a bit more confident, I took her aside when we left the room and said, "Here's the deal. I might not be able to carry things or do things exactly like all the other students. But if you want me to care for this patient, I promise you I can and I will do it, and it will be done flawlessly. I will crawl across the floor to get the job done, so please don't think there's anything I can't do."

I don't know if she believed me, but even the thought that she might doubt me had the same effect on me it always did: It only made me more determined.

Taking care of patients changes your life in a way you can't describe. Here I am complaining about sweating when I have to walk too far, and then I look in a room and I see a husband holding his wife's hand, wiping his tears away and saying how much he loves her. It makes my sweaty scrubs and sore legs meaningless. It makes me love my best friend and my family so much more, realizing that at any time that person in the hospital bed could be them—or me. I remember to smile more because patients need something to smile about. It makes me look at superheroes in a new light. A superhero to me used to be a Miss America or a Miss USA. Those women are still amazing to me, but now I see a superhero as someone like Michelle Roth, who goes out of her way to truly care and be there for patients. Superheroes are my mom and my grandmother, who take such loving care of their patients. Superheroes are the doctors I've known who answer emails from their patients no matter what time of day, or spend so much time and share so much knowledge that their patients feel fully informed and safe. They stay late and come in early to make sure you get seen when you want to be seen. I hope I can follow in the footsteps of these inspiring role models. I hope one day my patients think half as much of me as I do of the incredible health-care providers I have been lucky enough to know, both as a patient and as a student. Real superheroes don't wear red capes; they wear white coats, and only a few are brave enough to wear their hearts on their sleeves . . . and those are the greatest ones!

One reason I am so glad that I'm becoming a nurse practitioner is that it fits in with the two most basic things I believe:

You'll never know unless you try.

Always follow your heart and make your dreams a reality!

TWENTY-ONE
Miss You Can Do It

HBO released the *Miss You Can Do It* documentary in 2013. The result was exactly what I had hoped it would be: It put my little pageant on the map. Thanks to the documentary, we have reached people across the world, which means that more girls and their families will learn about the pageant. Hopefully, these girls and their families will be moved to take the same kind of chance I took back when I was in tenth grade and entered the Miss Henry County competition. To promote the documentary, HBO put together a publicity campaign, and one of the many things they arranged was for me to be interviewed for an article in *Vogue*. The *Vogue* photographer took a picture of me wearing a simple, elegant outfit of designer pants and a sleeveless blouse and used it for an article titled "Miss Congeniality: Abbey

Curran is changing the way we evaluate beauty, one unconventional pageant at a time." I love the title of that article because it summarizes exactly what I've been trying to do since I started Miss You Can Do It in tenth grade.

One of the reasons the pageant is still so important to me is that I have never lost sight of what it's like to have a challenge. I have been fortunate enough to have had some successes that most people don't have, but no amount of success will ever change the fact that when strangers see me limping down the street, I still hear them say, "That poor girl."

I hate being pitied as much as I hate being underestimated. Lately I've wondered if one reason people underestimate me is because I've been in beauty pageants—because although pageant girls get lots of special treatment, they don't get lots of respect. But whatever prejudices people may have about me because I've been a pageant girl are nothing—and I mean *nothing*—compared to the prejudice I still encounter all the time because I'm challenged. And I know that what's true for me is sadly true for all challenged people.

That's why one of my main inspirations for Miss You Can Do It is something one of the Miss USA judges told me, which I still think about every day. "We win things," she said, "only so we can pass the dream on to someone else." Those words changed my thinking forever. They made me realize that whenever I am pushing forward for me, I am also pushing forward for other girls with challenges.

That idea of passing on my dream defines the goal I have today. It's the reason I've worked so hard to make the pageant an event like no other. I truly am so grateful for the opportunity I've been given to encourage other girls with challenges and special needs, to help them realize for themselves what pageants taught me: No matter what anyone else thinks of you, no matter how much they discourage you, never give up and always follow your dreams. I also think it helps these girls to know about the enormous fears I had to face in order to compete in the Miss USA pageant. So I tell them about how I had to ignore the mean comments and not pay attention to all the people who assumed I would fail. I also tell them that pushing through those fears was worth it and that, because I realized my dream, I'm all the more excited about passing the dream on to them. I also want them to know what Shirley Cothran Barret, former Miss America, told me: that every accomplishment, small or great, begins with two words—"I'LL TRY!" I tell my girls, "Winning isn't everything, The thing that really counts is the effort we make. Win or lose, every time we try, we get stronger."

The planning for each year's pageant begins when we start accepting online entries from potential contestants through missyoucandoit.com. We start this process on Valentine's Day, and we always post on the website the phrase: "Fall in Love with Miss You Can Do It." I have to decide in advance on the number of contestants. Normally it's fifty, because that's a number we can accommodate without making the pageant ceremonies too long. But because of the documentary and the added publicity, we've had many more applicants in recent years, so I decided we could accept the first seventy-five girls to submit their online registration form and pay the $125 entry fee. You might think that we wouldn't have a fee, but the truth is we need to have one; all pageants have entry fees because pageant costs are huge, and the fees for Miss You Can Do It help us do everything that's required. The money is needed to bring special judges to Kewanee from places as far away as Los Angeles; it's needed for the purchase of the gorgeous decorations and sashes and crowns that create the magical world I want the girls to experience.

* * *

One thing that surprises a lot of people is that we don't ask the girls' parents to tell us about their child's particular challenge. That's because I think it would sound terrible if *What's your challenge?* was one of the questions on the entry form. Basically, it would be like asking, *What's wrong with you?* To me, it doesn't matter what a girl's challenge is. The pageant isn't about challenges; it's about overcoming them.

Every year we ask the girls, "If you could make one wish come true, what would it be and why?"

I've always found it interesting that so many of them tell us they would love to meet someone who stars in a Disney film or TV program. Because of that, I have tried and tried for many years to make that wish come true. And luckily, I was able to make that happen thanks to one of my good friends, Crystle Stewart, who was Miss Texas USA 2008 and was also the winner of the Miss USA pageant in 2008, the year I competed in it. She happens to be friends with a Disney producer who got us in contact with the agent of Sierra McCormick, a beautiful young actress who played one of the leads on the Disney series *A.N.T. Farm*.

When Sierra's agent called to say that Sierra was willing to come and be a judge at the 2014 Miss You Can Do It pageant, I was jumping up and down with excitement.

I posted the news on the Miss You Can Do It Facebook page and overnight it got dozens of likes. I was thrilled. One of the things I believe in is what I call the Circle of Dreams, which is the way one dream can lead to another. If I hadn't competed in the Miss USA pageant and made friends there, Sierra wouldn't be coming to my pageant. So because my dream came true, I would now be able to make the dreams of so many of my Miss You Can Do It girls come true by introducing them to Sierra.

Coming to rural Illinois is a lot of work. We don't have a direct flight from New York or Los Angeles (where most big names come from), and our local airports are so small that the planes that fly in here don't have a first class, which most celebrities require. Instead, you have to fly into Chicago and then someone has to pick you up and drive you the two hours to Kewanee. Now, for me, that's no big deal, but most celebrities want to land at the location they're traveling to. Sierra also wanted that, but once she was told it wasn't possible, she still agreed to come. Thank goodness!

The day before the actual pageant, we staged a huge princess party for all the girls at the home of Dr. Soderstrom, who has always been so supportive of the pageant and also of me. He's the one who saw to it that my preparation for the Miss Iowa and Miss USA pageants included lots of free facials and loads of pampering. He's been involved with the pageant for a few years, which really means a lot to me. He's helped us so much, both by donating money and by sending us makeup artists to do the faces of all the girls for free. His home is amazing: It's a genuine castle on a hill with turrets and stone walls and a big, beautiful lawn. Inside the house we arranged to have areas where the girls would have their hair and makeup done and where Dr. Soderstrom and I and some of the girls and their parents would be interviewed early in the day by TV and radio reporters. We always get a lot of reporters from different states who come to cover the pageant. This past year, we even had a reporter from a British women's magazine called *Bella*.

The party provided a perfect place to do the individual interviews with each of the girls that are part of the judging process, so we set up three big tables for the judges, with chairs for them on one side and a lone chair on the other side, where each girl would be seated when the judges interviewed her. Then right up the hill there were more tables all ready for a pizza party, and farther up, there was an ice-cream station with all sorts of flavors and toppings. Just beyond that there was a man making all different shapes of balloon animals. We also had some volunteers dressed up as Disney characters: Snow White and Sleeping Beauty and Cinderella and Princess Anna.

The girls loved every bit of it. Basically, we had seventy-two girls running wild, and each of them was assigned a hostess, which is a local person who volunteers to come to the pageant and help them. So that was 144 people right off the bat, not to mention the TV crews and the Soderstrom staff and the nine judges and our pageant helpers. It was so much fun, but pageant day had never been quite that chaotic.

The girls knew Sierra McCormick would be there, and that really was the thing that excited them the most. When she arrived at the Castle on Saturday, everyone and everything stopped. All of a sudden, the girls weren't interested in the beautiful Disney characters or the pizza or the ice cream. All they wanted to do was meet Sierra. It made me so happy to see all these sweet girls holding on to their walkers or walking in their little braces as they lined up for their private interview with the judges, where Sierra would actually be talking with them. I'd ask them, "Are you excited?" and they'd giggle and smile and so many of them told me they just wanted to hug Sierra.

Poor Sierra! She got up and down from her chair so many times to give those hugs, but it was so clear that she was happy to do it. Finally, I gave in and had to hug her, too, because I was so thrilled and grateful for the excitement and happiness she had brought to my lovely girls. I am a loyal fan of *A.N.T. Farm* now. I told her that when these girls go back to school and get made fun of or don't have any friends, they will have one thing that no one else in their school has: They will have Sierra McCormick as their friend. That made her cry, and when she cried, I did, too.

We also were very lucky to have Jenni Pulos, a producer at Bravo, as one of our judges. I had met her at the Most Inspirational Woman Awards a few years earlier in Los Angeles. I asked her if she would come to the pageant, and she has come for the last three years, even the year she'd had a baby less than a month before. She is such a sweet, kindhearted woman, and one of the funniest and most fun people I know. She raps and dances and gets everyone excited! The pageant just wouldn't be complete without Jenni.

These days, our pageant stage is absolutely gorgeous. We have huge crystal chandeliers. We have six shimmering crystal columns lining the back of the stage that change colors during the pageant from blue to turquoise to green to pink to purple. Then we have exquisite curtains made of crystals that fill the sides of the stage, the same exact ones the Miss USA state pageants use. When the girls see it for the first time, their jaws drop.

I was so happy just watching some of the girls backstage. You could see them pointing at Sierra, who was sitting in a seat positioned right in the center of the judges' table. The girls were just so excited to see her again and some of them would wave and wave from behind the curtain until Sierra waved back—and once she did, they had the biggest smiles you can ever imagine.

During the actual pageant, the girls do an opening number. Luckily, an awesome former college professor of mine, Katie Rushing Anderson, who teaches anatomy and physiology, also has a passion for kids with special needs and happens to be a dance teacher. So she choreographs an opening dance and teaches it to the girls at their rehearsal on Friday night, and then goes over it with them again about an hour before the doors open for the pageant. Then everyone competes in casualwear, evening gown, and the onstage question. It's only two outfit changes, but even with just that, the pageant still takes three to three and a half hours. It's a long night.

One of the contestants in our 2014 pageant was the most beautiful little girl with sparkling blue eyes and shiny blond hair. Her name is Reece. She really stood out. As she was being taken to her private interview with

Sierra McCormick, she tripped on the maxi dress she was wearing. I know she must have been just as mad at herself and embarrassed as I used to get—and still do on occasion. It was a pretty bad tumble, and if she had been a kid without a disability, she probably would have cried. But Reece knew better than to cry. Instead, she popped right back up and said, "Maxi dresses and leg braces just don't work together sometimes."

I was astonished by how she was able to keep her composure, and guess what? She ended up being our 2014 Little Miss You Can Do It Queen.

She was absolutely ecstatic, of course, but the great thing is that all the girls are excited beyond belief just to be in the pageant and to receive all the positive feedback and attention and love that we give them. At the very end of the evening, when Tina Turner's "Simply the Best" plays and the confetti falls and their pictures are projected onto the screen above the stage, what you see on the faces of all the girls is pure, undiluted joy. Some of the girls do not have long to live, and none of them will ever have what is considered a "normal" life. Yet their capacity for happiness, for living in the moment and appreciating everything they are given, are qualities that everyone can learn from. I understand how they feel because I felt that way when I stood on the stage at Miss

USA, and although I didn't win, I still felt wonderful and special and honored, and that's what I want to give these girls. I want them to have that moment in their lives that they will never, ever forget, a moment that will fill their hearts to bursting, so, for the rest of their lives, whenever they hear that song, they will be transported back to that place and time and those feelings, and their hearts will fill to bursting once more.

No matter what I do in the future, I am determined that the pageant will go on. We don't have a big sponsor, and every year the pageant grows, which means it costs more as well. If we don't find a big sponsor soon, I'll either need to open another credit card or start going door-to-door again, asking businesses for donations. I'd rather not do either of those things, but if they are the only way to keep the pageant running, I will.

My hope is that the pageant will grow to the level of Miss USA, which means there will be state pageants that feed into a national pageant. Another hope is that I could work with the contestants for a few weeks before the national pageant, just like the Miss USA competition does.

Someday, I hope we can move the pageant to a bigger venue, such as an incredible theater in New York

City or Los Angeles. And I hope to get more celebrities like Sierra McCormick who are willing to come and be pageant judges. How great would it be to fill my panel of judges with all the people the contestants dream of meeting!

One thing I know for sure is that the pageant has given me a reason far greater than myself to break glass ceilings, to make the world a better place for anyone born with a disability. Another thing I'm sure of is that my girls have given me far more than I have given them. They have given me a cause, a purpose, and even an identity—without these girls, I wouldn't be who I am today.

Because of the pageant, many other things have happened that have meant so much to me. For instance, one little girl who competed stole my heart. Her name is Mariel and she has dark brown hair, crystal-blue eyes, and pure white skin—she's so beautiful, she reminds me of Snow White. Like me, she has cerebral palsy and has trouble walking. She is so funny and full of life, and this past winter her mom asked me to come speak to her second-grade class for Career Day. I was a little nervous about talking to kids that young, but I was very surprised by what happened there. I started off by going around the room asking all of them what they want to be when they grow up. I got the usual: a doctor, a teacher, a veterinarian. Then a boy said he wanted to be a fashion designer. He asked if he could wear my crown and I let him; he then proceeded to tell me, in the nicest way, that he didn't like my gray sweater and that I would have looked better in red and that if he'd been at my house that morning he'd have done a better job pulling me together and doing my hair and my makeup. I said, "I'm sure you would have," and I smiled at him, thinking how amazing it was that he could say all this and no one in the class laughed at him. The next boy said that he wanted to be an NFL player. I asked him what team, what position, and then I asked the class, "How many of you think he can make it to the NFL?"

A little boy said, "All he needs to do is practice—he has a long time to practice." I agreed. And no one doubted him. Everyone thought he could achieve his dream. No one laughed at him and said, "Be realistic."

If we as adults could be like that second-grade class, the world would be a better place. I don't know when we start to make fun of other people's dreams and ambitions. I don't understand why people think they have the right to do that.

I truly believe this little boy can go to the NFL if people don't destroy his spirit before he gets there.

Another thing that happened that day was that Mariel

asked me to make sure I walked in front of her class so they would know she wasn't the only one who walks that way. So I said, "Okay, everyone, I am going to show you my walk, but please don't laugh at me and hopefully, after I show you, you'll still be my friends."

So I showed them my usual side-to-side herky-jerky walk, and no one laughed or made fun of me. And afterward, well, it melted my heart when another little boy raised his hand and said he would be my friend because it doesn't matter what's on the outside, it's what's on the inside that counts. At the end of the day, another little boy said he wanted me to wait there until his mom arrived. When I asked why he said it was because she would bring his piggy bank and give it to me. I asked why again and he said he was going to give me all of his money so I could go and get my walk fixed and then I wouldn't have to worry about it anymore. I fell so in love with those little angels that day. Why do we change? If grown men would act like those boys did, then maybe women like me would have a few dates before college. I was truly impressed with how smart and kind those kids were!

Today, my biggest dream is to change the world one girl at a time, one family at a time. I know that sounds cheesy, but it's needed. I've seen so many parents jump to conclusions about their child with special needs. They assume that their child can't do something before they even try. It breaks my heart.

I see it so often when I am with the Miss You Can Do It contestants. I notice that their parents are always very worried about them and they speak for them, telling me, "She can't do this or that." For example, this year, because the pageant was at the Castle, we couldn't invite the contestants' parents, family, and friends. That would have been way too many people. So we asked that the parents drop their daughters off and come back in a few hours to pick them up. Considering all the fun things we had for the girls to do, and the fact that our pageant crew and even health-care providers were on-site, there was really nothing to worry about. But even so, a lot of moms told me, "She can't do it. She can't go without me. She will be so upset."

In response, I always explain that each of the girls is accompanied by a reliable hostess who I select. And then I ask, "Have you ever let her try to go somewhere without you? I think she will be okay with Snow White and Cinderella, and pizza and balloons and an ice-cream truck." They never believe me, but they find out for themselves soon enough. It really makes me sad when parents don't allow their daughters to experience life on their own.

They think they are protecting their daughters, but it seems to me what they're really doing is depriving them of a life. This sort of overprotection may be meant well, but it makes the girls different, as if they come from another country where the language and customs are not like ours. I find that especially with my older girls. I can't really relate to them, and I believe that's because they are never without their parents. It's so important to have the freedom that allows you to make mistakes and learn from them. I think it's the only sure way to learn things; it's like if you touch your hand to a superhot stove— you're going to get burned and you're also going to figure out that you should never touch a hot stove again.

Girls who are sheltered like this don't make friends, and friends help you become who you want to be. Parents will guide you, but friends show you a different point of view, and I feel so bad that a lot of my girls miss out on that. I want them to go over to another girl's house and try on red lipstick and listen to whatever music they like and stay up as late as they please. Those kinds of experiences help you to become independent, to live a life that is your own, but my older girls never get to do them because they have become afraid to leave their parents even for one afternoon. They are afraid to try something their mother hasn't taught them.

As I type this book now, I am sitting in my nursing class waiting for a psychiatric mental health lecture to begin, and my friend Ali is sitting to my right keeping an eye out for when our professor walks by so I can minimize my computer screen. Now, I love my mother so much, but if she were with me, she would say, "Study, pay attention," and I know she's right and I'd do what she said. But I also know that sometimes studying can be saved for later. She'd also probably say, "Don't eat sticky candy, it's bad for your teeth," and I know that . . . but sometimes sticky candy can be fun, too.

I want my girls to find themselves. Experience life! Pick out their own clothes at the mall, choose whatever they want to eat, whatever movie they want to see. Most of them don't get to do that, and what they don't realize is that this becomes a whole other way of being disabled. When people make fun of them, I want them to be able to fight back, but you can't always do that when your parents are watching.

Recently, I went to the home of a little girl I know with CP to give her a birthday gift. She's another sweetheart, and I can see that she is very smart and has hopes and dreams. Her CP is more severe than mine. She uses a wheelchair and she sits in an automatic device to get up stairs, but her mind is perfect and she is precious! I feel so bad for her, because although she is blessed to have a mother who loves and cares for her, at the same time her mother doesn't always encourage her to be more independent or confident.

I have seen her fly across the floor on her hands and knees. And I mean fly! So if it were me, my parents would let me fly up and down the stairs. It doesn't matter if you crawl up them and go down them on your butt, like I used to do. When I was her age I had my Barbie car to get around in and I had my parents' okay to crawl around the floor.

I also had my Hello Kitty push toy to lean on, and even though it was hard to walk, I managed to do it. Walking can be so difficult when you have CP—it makes you sweat, that's for sure—but I think this girl should be encouraged to try. I honestly don't think she needs a wheelchair, either. What she needs is to be allowed some independence, which will give her the confidence that there are many things she can do for herself.

I get so mad and sad every time I see the way her mother doubts her at times, even though I realize she has only the best of intentions. One day when I went over to her house for a visit, her mother asked why I was dressed the way I was. I was wearing black leggings and tennis shoes and a purple tank top and a black sports bra and my hair was in a ponytail and I had a black sweatband on my head. I actually dress like that a lot of the time, but I guess she had only seen me when I was dressed up. I told her that I had just finished doing a spin class. I'm in love with spin class. I've finally found a workout I can do just as well, if not better, than other people. But this mother said, right in front of her daughter, "Oh, I don't think she'll ever be able to do that." This little girl still has her whole life in front of her!

So I said, "Of course she could do spin class someday; anyone can do anything if they want it bad enough!"

If this precious girl was my daughter, I would teach her to look up at the moon and the stars and tell her that she has this whole big world to conquer and that with every star she has an opportunity to make a wish. I would tell that we never know unless we try, and that she's beautiful and she's smart and can do things, and that she makes me proud. I have told her those things, and I keep hoping I can help her; I want to so much.

I also hope the Miss You Can Do It pageant opens the eyes of all the contestants' parents and shows them that their children are way more capable than they could ever imagine! That's why I insist that the girls do everything we have lined up for them: answer questions in front of the judges' panel, walk onto the stage with one of our escorts, answer the onstage question, learn and perform the opening dance number. You have to do everything and that's only because I know you can!

Some of the moms have told me beforehand, "My daughter can't do that." And I don't want to be mean, but I have to tell them, "Well, then this is the wrong pageant for her, because we are called Miss You CAN Do It." Most of the time, the parents give in, and then they are so surprised and pleased when they see that, in fact, their daughters can do it.

We are strict at the pageant because we believe in the girls. For instance, when it comes time for their interview with the judges, we make the girls do it alone. The interviews are held in a room and no one is allowed to go in with them. It's just them and the judges. Every year before the pageant begins, I get emails from a lot of parents saying something like, "My daughter is scared to walk with strangers, so my husband will sit in the front row of the pageant and jump onstage and walk with her." Ummm, no! Your daughter is completely capable of walking with the escorts the pageant provides for her.

Or they'll write, "My daughter can't do an opening dance number." Well, in my pageant I don't care about if they can or not—they sure as heck are going to try.

That's the point. Don't tell me what these girls can and can't do. Most don't have the slightest idea what they can do because they haven't been given the chance to do much of anything. I also hope it shows the girls that they don't have to care what anyone else thinks—even if that person is their mother! I tell them, "You are amazing . . . You are beautiful . . . and even if you want to do something that has never been done before, that doesn't mean it's not possible."

Today, thousands of girls, most of whom I have never even met, are looking up to me. They tweet me, email me, Facebook me. They say all kinds of things, mostly about their disabilities and about how they are different physically and how different they feel—and I understand every one of their emotions. Each girl has a specific situation, but what they all have in common is that they are afraid. So I can't be afraid, I can't let something get the best of me, because when I reply to them, it's to tell them to not be afraid. I need to set the example. Each moment of my life I think of them. And because of them, I'm not afraid of anything.

Well, to be perfectly honest, sometimes I am afraid. But I refuse to let it stop me! But stronger than any fear of what others might think is my belief in taking risks, in being brave; it's about showing myself and everyone else that I can do anything I set my mind to.

I want my girls to be brave. My goal is to reach them before they become convinced that they don't have what it takes. So what I always tell them is, "You just have to be brave enough to try, because unless we try, we don't have any idea of all the things we can do. You might be the outcast and feel like a loser and feel afraid of other people's opinions. But you need to stand up and ignore their shallow and negative thoughts. Just go out there and make history and prove them wrong!"

The best thing that has happened to me is that I no longer see having CP as something horrible; I don't need to pray for God to ease my pain. I see now that cerebral palsy can be a blessing. It has taken me on a path I never could have even imagined. These days, every time I leave the house for a long trip or in bad weather, my mother says, "Please, please don't die." I always say, "Don't be sad if I do . . . know that I died happy."

One thing that has made me very happy is that recently my grandma Wink bought me a pony, because she said she knows that Grandpa Jack would have wanted me to have it. This beautiful pony is a mini-mare, and I decided that I would donate her for the winters to New

Kingdom Trail Riders, which is a great organization that uses horses in therapeutic programs for special-needs individuals and military veterans. I hope the girls who get to ride her have as much fun on her as I had riding my pony Crackers when I was a little girl.

Today, I am living proof that believing in yourself makes all the difference in the world. It's not that I'm without insecurities. I still have plenty. I still have never walked into a room and thought I was the coolest or the smartest or the prettiest person there. I wish I knew what that felt like, but I don't. The point is—and this is what I tell the Miss You Can Do It girls—I walk into the room anyway.

And I'm okay with lacking some confidence, because I never want to think I'm better than someone else. I'm not. We all make mistakes, we all have bad days, and the bottom line is, we all need someone at times.

Another thing I pass on to the Miss You Can Do It girls is a saying I found on a plaque hanging in the Kewanee farm store: *Life is not about waiting for the storm to pass; it's about learning to dance in the rain.*

All of us have moments when we are looking to take shelter and wait for the rain to stop. My hope is that this book will encourage others to do what I have learned to do: Take a chance and face the storm.